Acknowledgments

Many people were involved with the creation of this book, and I wish I could write a paragraph about each of them. In many cases, I can only provide a listing of names, which does not do justice to the contributions made.

Kali entered my life thanks to Judy Anderson and stimulated the creative glimmer that ultimately became this book. As the idea began to take form, Kay Fritzsche acted as my sounding board and Rosario Martinez-Cañas offered her seemingly unlimited creative vision. Joyce Leake published an article and two of my stories, each illustrated by Sarah Skeen, in her online magazine, "Living with Animals: Stories of People and Animals," and the favorable response to those endeavors provided the impetus I needed.

My dream took flight the day Susan Chernak McElroy, one of my favorite authors, wrote to say that she'd be happy to contribute a story. That marvelous news was followed by an uplifting message from agent Andrea Hurst, saying Dr. Bernie Siegel would love to have Smudge's story included.

The effort was further boosted when Faith Maloney, a founder of Best Friends Animal Society, offered her friendship and support. Then Caroline Gilbert, founder and manager of The Fund for Animals Rabbit Sanctuary, and Erika Smith Royal, founder and president of Brambley Hedge Rabbit Rescue, agreed to participate. Members of the Colorado House Rabbit Society also offered their stories.

Encouraging words came from others as well. Joanne Lauck, whose friendship and work I greatly value, helped in countless ways. Author Amelia Kinkade and Michael Markarian, president of The Fund for Animals, offered inspiring thoughts and support. So did two new friends: T. J. Banks and Rita Reynolds, fellow animal lovers and authors. Others who deserve mention include: J. Kirby Bivans, Max Bruce, Ann Cahoy, the late Mary Ann Capra, Dr. Gabriel Cousens, Maggy Cuesta, Kristin Des Marais, Jasmine Estrada, the late Nathania

Gartman, Anna Horton, Dr. C. Yashpal Jayne, Dr. Terry Moore, Linda Radke and her staff, Ellen Reid, Sister Maryam, Kelly Thornsley, Diane Young, and Liga Zvirgzdina.

As the process unfolded, Kali remained my constant inspiration, and many wonderful veterinarians and rabbit-knowledgeable people assisted me in caring for her. Dr. Jerry LaBonde was our primary support during the first difficult months. We were also very fortunate to work with other skilled veterinarians: Drs. Paula Bumpers, Laura George, Bill Guerrera, Donald Holmes, William Kurmes (and practice manager, Melanie), and Dave Nicholson. Others who helped me include Pam Beets, Karen Green, Dana Krempels, Bea LeNoir, and Kathleen Wilkens. I'll always be grateful to Sue Green for putting me in touch with Connie Conine, whose knowledge of rabbits and background in occupational therapy proved invaluable. Others who lent a hand include Amanda Gorski, Kim Khatibi, Kathryn Nelson, Linda Palmer, Savannah Sydney, and Dani Scanland. Special thanks also go to Michele and Tony Hill and their son, Troy, for sharing their tales and for helping save the lives of two bunnies who now reside with us.

I was delighted when Nancy LaRoche shared her love and knowledge of rabbits by contributing two stories and agreeing to collaborate on the project. In addition, it was a great pleasure and privilege to work with the generous individuals who shared information about their rabbits. I'm also sincerely grateful for the contributions of each of the talented artists and photographers mentioned throughout the book, including Beverly Endsley, who supports rabbit rescue in myriad ways. Valuable suggestions from the pre-publication readers improved the text, and I thank: Joan Carstensen, Susan Gossman, Dee Heinrich, and Kathy Stevens. A sincere note of thanks also goes to Nora Ernst, Edith Hathaway, Anita Kerr, Pam Laverty, Christine Schrock, Howard Voeks, Victoria Walton, and Alissa Witzke.

The stories and educational pieces became what they are through the efforts of Karen Witzke. Her respect for animals as well as her knowledge of the English language are apparent on every page. I am very grateful for her precision, style, and friendship.

The final manuscript came together with the assistance of Lucile Moore, who contributed an educational article and very graciously helped me meet deadlines. Dr. Vittorio Capello, Margo DeMello, and Dr. Angela Lennox offered their extensive knowledge, helping to make this book more accurate and complete; Dr. Lennox also contributed an educational article. James Wallace, president of the Society for the Preservation of English Language and Literature (SPELL), contributed editorial expertise. Lloyd Rich, publishing attorney, gave important legal guidance.

Andrea Hurst of Andrea Hurst Literary Management was my consultant, and I appreciate her professionalism, patience, and humor. Dan Poynter, through his writings, provided invaluable information about book publishing. Rudy Ramos of Rudy Ramos Design Studio created the perfect design and made the process easy and enjoyable.

That Dr. Michael W. Fox agreed to write the Foreword to this book is a heartfelt honor. His were the first books

I read when searching for answers about the behavior of a rescued cat, and he continues to be an inspiration to me. Dr. Fox's compassion, respect, and love extend to all beings and are very evident in all that he does.

I'm deeply grateful to the following individuals who read the manuscript and offered review comments: Susana M. Della Maddalena, Margo DeMello, Marinell Harriman, Kiska Icard, Dr. Elliot M. Katz, Amelia Kinkade, Joanne Lauck, Diana Orr Leggett, Dr. Angela M. Lennox, Michael Markarian, Jeffrey Masson, Jeanne McCarty, Bari Mears, Lucile C. Moore, Mary Lou Randour, Tom Regan, Rita Reynolds, Erika Smith Royal, Dr. Allen M. Schoen, Kenneth Shapiro, and Susan Taylor.

My final words of gratitude are for my father, the late Donald Grosshuesch, who recognized and loved Kali's tremendous spirit and independence; my mother, Audrey Grosshuesch, who edited early versions of the stories and offers unfailing moral support; my uncle, Vernon Wernecke, who understands how important the animals are to me and remembers to ask about them; and John Mead, dear friend and fellow animal lover, whose support helped make my dream a reality.

Author's Note

None of the stories in this book refer to a rabbit's "owner," a term which suggests that companion animals are property—relegated to the level of *things* and dealt with according to our desires. Instead, the word "guardian" is frequently used, interspersed with "human companion" and "caregiver" when those words better fit the story.

"Guardian" captures the best parts of humans' relationships with other animals, implying that creatures deserve to be treated with respect, compassion, and love because all animals are sentient beings and have inherent value. A guardian protects his or her dependent companions, honoring each animal's individuality and properly providing for physical, social, and emotional needs during the animal's lifetime.

Reference the Resource (Services) section for information on the Guardian Campaign.

FOREWORD

The first animal whom I ever learned to hold properly, and trust and love, was my little bunny rabbit named Thumper. He was a black-and-white Dutch dwarf, but he was huge to me, filling my arms as he relaxed, feeling through his body my trust and lack of fearful tension. He was a gentle rabbit, never once biting me for being a somewhat clumsy and not yet very empathetic four-year-old.

My father built a beautiful big hutch for Thumper and set it in the back garden, protectively against the rear wall of our garage. I fed my rabbit and cleaned his hutch every day, always talking to him about the important topics and questions that filled my young mind.

I do not remember how long he lived, but I do recall the morning when I found my bunny friend lying unresponsive on his side. The night before he'd been alive and full of frisk so I was bewildered, waiting for his ears to move and nose to twitch as I called his name. Being too afraid to put a hand on him, I probed Thumper gently with a stick, wishing his spirit to return to his lifeless form. When I did eventually touch him, he was cold and stiff as wood. That was my first lesson in death and loss.

Just days later, while in the garden lush with flowers and insects and still wondering about life and death and worried about where Thumper had gone, I had an experience that was quite a surprise to me at my young age. I was looking skyward, through the English-morning mist, when everything became bathed in light. I transformed into a tiny particle, no longer a separate entity but instead clearly connected to the whole of life. I could feel Thumper's warmth and gentleness as he, too, was part of that infinite love and light. My fear of death departed, and my sense of who I was changed. I saw the world filled with other lives and forms of being, all distinctly joined to me and to one another and, thanks to a small rabbit, I saw them with great clarity and with everlasting awe. That experience has stayed fresh in my mind ever since because of what Thumper gave me in life and in death.

But though Thumper taught me such a profound lesson, it was wrong of us to have denied him any contact with his own kind during his life with us. He never had the chance to know what it is to be a rabbit and to be the soul-mirror of another in his form and state of mind. Rabbits, along with all other beings, have the right to live in harmony with their nature. They have a life and a will of their own, independent of our lives, interests, and needs.

I feel a terrible loneliness when I contemplate the existence and fate of millions of rabbits who live alone in tiny cages for their entire lives, unable to stretch out fully, move freely, or enjoy the life they were meant to have. Such treatment reveals our ignorance, callous indifference, and rabbit blindness. Whenever I think of this and about how disconnected we've become from nature, I fear what our children are learning. What is the likely outcome when we, as adults, model a lack of awareness of the inherent value of other creatures and a lack of concern about the quality of their lives?

Most of us would agree that pets have the right to a good home. But rabbits are unlike the cats and dogs with which we are so familiar, and our lack of knowledge too often means that the rabbits' needs are ignored. They were meant to live with other bunnies, playing all kinds of inventive games of speed and deception, determining their rank, engaging in grooming rituals, and caring for one another. Though selective breeding has made them less fearful and also dependent upon humans for safety and care, domestic rabbits can still enjoy warren life, though their "warren" may look quite different from that of a wild rabbit and may include, in addition to bunny companions, a human, cat, and dog. When humans establish a participatory relationship with their rabbits, they come closer to experiencing harmony with their essential self and all of the living earth.

Some of the beauty of my pet bunny is reflected in the beauty of this book, in the personal stories of human discovery, of living with rabbits, and of a rabbit's true and wonderful nature. As you will read, they are highly sociable, communicative, empathetic, intelligent, responsive, and readily trainable. The sciences of ethology and biology have helped deepen our understanding and appreciation of rabbits, and this important book takes us one step further. The intimate accounts of people's experiences with rabbits, which could never be replicated in a research laboratory, bring to conscious realization all that a rabbit is.

I urge you, when reading this book, to think about the suffering and deaths of untold numbers of rabbits who, every year, are used to test cosmetics, deodorants, and other products. No animal should ever be made to suffer partial blindness in testing a new mascara or to die from cancer because we refuse the wisdom of organic agriculture. There are many safe, natural, organic botanical products, including medicinal ones, readily available on the open market that do not victimize these creatures.

I believe that an animal-exploiting consumerism, which I equate with the inability to see the value in all life, must be replaced by a change of heart—opening to the angelic innocence of rabbits, knowing them as unique individuals, and seeing reflected in their eyes the ancient depth of being that moves us to realize the sanctity of all life.

Rabbits and other animals provide a link with nature, nourishing our own souls. In the wild, they are vital contributors to the health of eco-systems—meadows, grasslands, heaths, moors, steppes—being in co-evolved, mutually enhancing symbioses with the ground vegetation and, therefore, with the dependent insect, bird, and reptile populations. On many organically certified farms, rabbits and other furred, feathered, and scaled beings are welcome participants in the endeavors of my human friends and associates who are able to see as Thumper taught me to see. Together, they give CPR to the Earth—conservation, preservation, and restoration.

The worldview of rabbits is revealed in some detail in this book, along with the rabbit's basic environmental, social, and emotional needs. This will go a long way to enhance our respect for rabbits as feeling beings, who are in many ways more similar to us than they are different. In addition, because some people need to be educated toward greater empathy and others need to be educated toward greater responsibility, the information in this book will also help improve the care rabbits receive from their not-always-well-informed humans.

We can learn much from rabbits, if we but take the time to observe and learn. They are sensitive beings who are uninhibited and honest in their emotions and responses, and we would do well to emulate such authenticity.

Flash an intense light on a rabbit and she will freeze, an easy target for the hunter. Flash the light on how we humans mistreat other living beings and we also freeze. Let us flash the light in a new direction, as a beacon toward a more compassionate age—one in which this book, Thumper, and all animals can teach us how to live in connection with all life.

Humility, compassion, respect, and reverence for all living things are the keys to a just, humane, and sustainable society. It is time to move and to embrace the whole of Creation.

—Michael W. Fox, DSc, PhD, BVetMed, MRCVS

INTRODUCTION

*Her name was Kali, and she taught me
lessons that transcended my usual boundaries.
She happened to be a rabbit.*

My important life lessons have often arrived in an unexpected manner, and most of the teachings have come from animal-friends. So it was with Kali.

She was a small rabbit, weighing less than four pounds. From the moment she arrived in our home, Kali commanded my attention. She'd been removed from a pre-school classroom, where she suffered neglect and had become very ill. And yet she brimmed with personality, confidence, and self-will.

I was instantly captivated and promised Kali I'd do my best to provide good care. At the time, my husband, John, and I knew nothing about tending house rabbits. Our interactions, if they can be called that, had been limited to intermittent observations of wild rabbits. In hindsight, I know that if we had needed to qualify as potential adopters, John and I would have failed due to our lack of knowledge—about rabbits in general and especially about domestic bunnies with myriad health considerations, like Kali.

Though John and I had rescued many abused and injured animals, Kali was the first with such permanent and extensive needs. Caring for her became a special gift—a perfect conduit for my development on the sometimes-arduous journey toward personal wholeness. I had to think and do things differently, to turn inward and find creative ways to help her overcome hurdles. In doing so, I overcame some of my own.

At the time, my father was in declining health. He and I had a close—though difficult—relationship. Through working with Kali, I came to truly know compassion, empathy, and awe. Although I thought I was already aware of the depth and meaning of these life-enhancing emotions, I soon realized that I had only touched their surface. Kali opened me to the intensity of those feelings; because of her I began to understand and interact with my aging father on a much deeper level than would have been possible otherwise. In short, what I learned from Kali made me a more sensitive and respectful person.

As I tended her, I pondered the very different lesson the impressionable children at the preschool had inadvertently learned: that it was okay to neglect and mistreat a classroom pet. My concerns led to writing an article (appearing at the back of this volume) discussing the divergent needs of children and rabbits. That effort was the beginning of the process that ultimately created this book.

While researching rabbits in order to understand Kali and her needs, I learned about the plight of many domestic rabbits: neglected in small cages or backyard hutches, living without companionship, and often euthanized because of a lack of understanding about their temperament and needs.

In sharp contrast, I met people who were enamored of rabbits and who were willing to share their living spaces in ways that allowed the companion rabbits to express their true natures. Those were the people who smiled knowingly whenever I shared something special about Kali.

I wanted to collect and write stories about those rabbits—the ones who were given freedom and allowed to exhibit the full panorama of their intricate personalities. I contacted Susan Chernak McElroy and Dr. Bernie Siegel, both of whom generously agreed to contribute to the project. I also queried rescue organizations—dedicated folks who work daily to help educate others about the temperament and proper care of rabbits—for their true stories. And I wrote "Stardust" to capture Kali's story, including what a blessing she has been in my life. This book contains many of those stories. Even though some of the rabbits portrayed in the following pages endured sad beginnings, all the bunnies ended up in wonderful homes, living very happy lives.

I had planned to give Kali a copy of "her book" (as I've always considered it) even though I know she would have simply turned it into a napping spot. But just before this book could be printed, Kali let me know it was time for her to depart this life. She remains in my heart, and she visits me during quiet contemplation and in my dreams, always demanding my attention. Other times I imagine her sitting on my father's lap, reading together—the idea brings me quiet joy.

I continue to be amazed and humbled by what I have learned from rabbits, small unassuming creatures that they are. In truth, Kali was small in physical size only. She graced my life with her formidable presence, allowing me to grow in wisdom and strength. What I learned from her emphasizes the unity of all life and transcends the barriers that too often exist between humans and various species of other animals.

Kali remains my teacher, my inspiration, and the catalyst for this book. She is not the only rabbit who has shared our household, but she was my first and she has blessed my life in numerous ways. For each moment with her, I am grateful.

MARIE MEAD

STARDUST

I wasn't expecting *her*.

I'm not sure who or what I was expecting, exactly—maybe a familiar rabbit from my childhood: the wild brown ones with cotton-ball tails and cute upright ears, who danced through grass fields decorated with clover and raced ahead of me in corn fields where I played hide-and-seek.

Those were the rabbits of my youth, and I knew back then that the very act of witnessing their *aliveness* would bring me luck. Each full moon I'd watch, hoping to glimpse one of them leap into the air, stardust trailing behind as she carried my dreams to the heavens.

On those visions hinged my presumptions about all rabbits, including the domestic rabbit for whom we agreed to provide a home.

My husband, John, and I had twenty-four hours to prepare for his arrival. We were told we'd be receiving a healthy six-month-old male rabbit with "behavior problems." He had been dismissed from a preschool classroom after lunging at a child who was trying to pet him through the wire cage.

We knew nothing about living with a domestic rabbit, so I did some quick preparations: found a rabbit veterinarian, obtained dietary guidelines, and checked out the two available library books. An expeditious shopping trip, a rapid perusal of the books, and we were as ready as we would be. At least the rabbit would be young and healthy—that meant there would be time to research and learn as we went along.

His arrival at 7:00 p.m. kicked holes in any expectations I might have had. Instead of a sleek brown rabbit with upright ears, the small cage held a black, long-haired rabbit with lop ears partially shielding dull, expressionless eyes.

I kept looking for the *aliveness*—but there didn't seem to be any. No fire, no vigor, not a glimmer of hope. Definitely no stardust.

Afraid to touch him and unable to voice my concerns, I simply stared. Surely there was some mistake.

But there wasn't.

A horrid, sinking feeling settled in my stomach. This was not the rabbit I was expecting. He was anything but healthy. Or happy. His very *essence* was missing.

The long Angora fur, thin and lackluster, hid his feet and belly. I thought I should pick him up and check his body—for lumps, bumps, *something*. Caution immediately intervened: *Be careful. You know virtually nothing about rabbits. You might injure him.* I had read enough to know that, if held improperly, injuring him was a probability, and a high one at that.

What was the matter with him? John and I kept staring, trying to discern any problems. As rabbit novices, we would have recognized only glaring health issues, and we saw nothing of the sort.

We couldn't help but *smell* a problem, though. A terrible stench had accompanied the bunny into the house, so we turned our attention to the wire cage—his "home" at the school—filthy with hardened diarrhea and urine.

After guiding him into a clean cat carrier, we discarded soiled cedar shavings; pried feces off the wire; sanitized the cage; scrubbed the slime-filled water bottle and food container; and threw out the unhealthy mix of green cereal, dried beans, and seeds. Then we put a cotton towel over a portion of the wire floor and ushered him back into his cage.

"After we get home from the vet's office tomorrow, I'll go shopping for the best rabbit house available," I promised.

There was no indication he heard me. But he did nibble the food purchased earlier that day, and we thought that was a good sign.

The next morning I waited with him for the animal clinic to open. It didn't take long for the veterinarian to complete the exam and give me the shocking news: we had rescued a two-and-a-half-year-old female bunny.

And she was dying.

"Her condition is so critical that even with medication and hydration she may not recover," the veterinarian advised. "She's severely malnourished, underweight, and in severe pain."

That wasn't all. Our new family member had a serious bladder infection and exhibited signs of gastrointestinal stasis, a painful killer of rabbits. As a result of living on a wire floor for so long, she had broken toes; sores on the bottom of her misshapen feet; improperly growing toenails, some more than two inches long; and weak, undeveloped leg muscles. The phenols from the cedar shavings made her susceptible to respiratory and liver problems, while the strong ammonia fumes from her urine-soaked cage might create additional health concerns.

When pressed to give a prognosis, the vet conceded, "Perhaps a week."

I drove home in a daze. *The poor little rabbit is dying. How could someone not notice?* Those were the only coherent thoughts that drummed in my head. And then it dawned on me: *She was in pain; that's why she lunged at the child.*

I hated putting her back into that wire cage, but it was all we had. "Just a few more hours and you'll have a new house, one *without* a wire floor." It didn't matter how short a time she might live, John and I weren't about to let her remain in the cage that had so damaged her body.

By mid-afternoon, a three-story rabbit condo was set up in our living room, and our resident bunny was placed inside. John made a short, carpet-covered ramp so Kali, as we named her, could more easily enter and exit her new abode. He also attached a roomy pen to keep our fragile little prey animal safe until our cats accepted her as a valued member of the family.

As soon as John opened her door, Kali stumbled down the low incline, nipping my hand when I tried to assist her. Her withered muscles allowed no more than an uncertain lurching movement. But her spirit, previously imprisoned as surely as if an iron mantle had been clamped around it, soared—*aliveness* shone from Kali's black-brown eyes. Her body tired quickly, but her eyes remained bright.

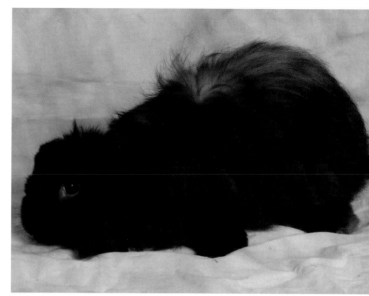

Bill Reed Photography

However, when we closed her inside her new house, to ensure her safety while we slept, Kali underwent a dramatic change. She began banging her head against the door, over and over. Alarmed that she might injure herself, John opened the door; she immediately stopped, remaining in front of the opening.

He closed it again, knowing we couldn't take the chance that one of our cats might harm her.

Kali again banged her head against the door. She didn't want out; she just didn't want to be shut in.

"We'll open it first thing in the morning," I assured her.

Kali's eyes lost their sparkle. She moved into a corner of her lodging, lay down, and turned her head away.

The aliveness was gone; it was as though we were watching her die.

Perhaps we were, and it frightened me.

Kali's misery was like a lead weight, so heavy and tangible that it followed us to bed. Finally, unable to sleep, I returned to the living room and opened the door to her condo, reading and maintaining vigil until morning.

The next couple of days were the same. I scrutinized her movements, trying to find signs of improvement. But her condition remained critical.

As we passed the one-week mark, it seemed Kali was responding to the medical treatment, although she remained in serious condition, straddling life and death. I was in contact with respected veterinarians, with the House Rabbit Society, and with others who knew rabbits. Instead of a learn-as-we-go situation, John and I were getting a crash course in health crises and medical treatment. But we were willing and committed students.

On her good days, she refused to remain in her condo. I'd open the play area and let her roam the house, allowing her to exercise her weak muscles as much as possible. The cats recognized Kali's substantial and forceful spirit and, even though she could not hop or run, they would back away when she slithered her way across the room.

Three weeks passed, and she was still alive.

November segued into the holiday season. At almost six weeks, her legs strengthened and she began hopping, albeit in an unsteady fashion. She was a feisty little thing, applying her right to freedom no matter how often she ended up spread-eagle on the floor.

But all was not well.

New concerns continued to surface. It was as though we peeled away one layer of health problems only to reveal another.

Kali's long black coat was often soaked with urine. I knew urine burn could be a serious problem and tried all the standard methods for keeping an incontinent rabbit dry. The vet ruled out a recurring bladder infection. Others suggested that Kali either had a behavior problem or was stressed due to the cats.

Intuition told me it was neither.

I researched, including textbooks containing medical information about rabbits. Nothing enlightened me.

Then Kali intermittently began losing her balance. X-rays revealed an active case of arthritis in her pelvis and legs. Every movement was painful.

A course of anti-inflammatory drugs, and Kali was able to move more easily and to actually squat while urinating. She continued to falter and end up on her nose, but she was getting stronger—and more independent.

I was hopeful that Kali was healing.

But then, nearly two months after she arrived at our home, the incontinence returned, caused by an improperly working bladder sphincter. And, despite the management of her arthritis, her balance problems returned. She didn't have a bacterial or viral infection, so I wondered if her vision was impaired or whether the third eyelids, which would sometimes partially close, were the cause of problems.

Continued consultations with veterinarians were helpful: Kali suffered from anemia, improperly functioning third eyelids, and probable neuromuscular damage that would cause ongoing difficulties.

Her early living conditions were taking their toll.

The New Year arrived, with Kali thumping it in. *Thump, thump, thump.* I knew this behavior, which had escalated over the weeks, was a symptom, but I couldn't discover the cause.

Even though I worked from home and could provide regular care, it became increasingly difficult for me to tend Kali. John and I were managing her health issues, but there was still something else wrong, something not yet detected. I could feel it.

But I didn't know how to find it.

One morning her soft, black coat was dripping with urine. I'd been able to keep her delicate skin dry up to this point, but the problem was worsening and I knew something had to be done before her skin became painfully inflamed and blistered.

Finally, I had to admit that being captivated by Kali and wanting to give her a home weren't enough. John and I just didn't know enough to tend a rabbit with so many special needs.

I feared we'd have to relinquish her. The misery was a savage lock around my heart. "Kali, I don't know how to take care of you," I hiccupped between sobs.

I renewed my efforts at calling people, trying to find someone who would spend time at the house and teach me more. I remember one phone call in particular: after hearing about our situation, the person suggested it might be kinder to euthanize Kali.

Euthanize Kali?

I could barely comprehend the words. They were like metal shards colliding in my head.

Kali was stronger in spirit than anyone I knew. Sure, she had some physical limitations, but that never stopped her. I thought of her as perfect, despite her myriad health issues.

That night, Kali's spirit charged through the midnight silence and into my dreams.

Before I could stop her, she proudly leaped through the underside of puff-cheeked clouds.

I followed, afraid she might fall. But then my eyes saw as hers did, and I wasn't frightened for her anymore. Kali hopped with certainty over the sea of clouds, to horizon's edge.

I was in awe. Her legs worked—she was frisking about like a young colt! THIS was her reality, one where there were no boundaries, no rules, no restrictions.

I watched from a distance, wanting to remain out of sight, afraid my presence might be an intrusion that would dispel the miracle.

Then Kali turned and looked right at me. I realized she had known I was nearby all the time. She seemed at ease with me.

She started to come toward me. An acrobat, she bounded through the heavens. I was so happy she was coming to me, and I opened my arms to receive her.

Just that quickly she leaped—

The frantic barking of neighborhood dogs yanked me back into the bedroom, wide awake.

What did my dream mean? Had Kali died during the night?

I raced into the living room. There she was, dark eyes sparkling.

I sat with her and answers began coming. I realized my fears for her had become obstacles in my way. John and I had rescued many animals before but never a rabbit, so I had not trusted my instincts.

But I *knew* and understood Kali. I loved her and wanted to keep her with us.

I made more phone calls, seeking answers. And they came, in the form of a wonderful and generous occupational therapist who had lived with a rabbit. Connie came to the house and observed Kali. She listened as I described patterns and the behaviors that seemed out of place.

Then she lay down on the floor with me to watch Kali move around. Connie immediately detected a slight imbalance in Kali's hind legs—one leg was doing a majority of the work. Because of the Angora fur it wasn't easy to see, but Kali's front legs weren't working properly either. Severely splayed, they were unable to support her weight and only helped steer about. When our intrepid rabbit came to rest, the forelegs became like fins, sliding back alongside her body.

This was something no one had seen before because Kali would always sit with her back legs pushed forward—a response to weak muscles and arthritis, we thought, but in actuality also a way to keep her front legs in place and to remain upright. Now Kali was strong enough to hold her body in position, revealing one strong hind leg, one weak hind leg, and two impaired front legs. That helped explain her balance issues and her ineffective stance when urinating.

Connie demonstrated simple exercises to help strengthen Kali's muscles—like holding my hand against one side of her body so that she'd have to lean differently—and provided simple, creative solutions for keeping fur dry while ensuring safe footing.

And then another perceptive person visited us. Karen's

Bill Reed Photography

knowledge of rabbits made it easy for her to confirm what I already suspected: Kali was deaf.

Ah, the last piece of the puzzle. Since Kali couldn't hear and because her vision was sometimes obscured by wayward third eyelids, she startled easily and thumped her distress.

Everything seemed so easy after that. No longer was I tentative when I needed to be assertive. I felt confident as John and I worked together to assist our precious rabbit.

Her muscles began to build; her back legs began working in tandem. She still hopped in an unsteady, lopsided fashion, but getting around was easier.

I started communicating with hand signals, and Kali responded.

She knew we were doing our best and began trusting us.

It was during this time that my father began showing serious signs of decline. His body, once strong, was aging rapidly. He shared his fears, especially about his memory loss, but I didn't have the knowledge—or patience at times—to assist him in all the ways he required. The fact that he resided in another state compounded the problem, so I arranged for others to accommodate his needs.

My life was just becoming routine again when, without warning, respiratory illness struck Kali. Her system shut down so quickly that she went into gastrointestinal stasis. I administered the prescribed medication, kept her body temperature stable, and hydrated and syringe-fed her, but death seemed imminent.

I held her, watching small breaths labor in and out.

Then she stopped breathing.

I did too. Tears streamed from my eyes. I wasn't ready to let her go.

I felt her body spasm. She started breathing again. Little short breaths, but she was breathing.

That night I had the same dream as before, but this time I saw the leap—

Kali started to come toward me. An acrobat, she bounded through the heavens. I was so happy she was coming to me, and I opened my arms to receive her.

Just that quickly she leaped, stardust showering over me as she ascended to the stars.

I startled awake. *Kali.* I hurried to make sure she was all right and was relieved to see her near-black eyes watching for me.

Kali gained enough weight to tip the scales at nearly four pounds. As she became stronger, she also came fully into her true self: a brave, spirited, dauntless, volitional, impertinent rabbit.

She was often indignant, even belligerent. If I was in her path, she'd slap her tiny feet rapidly against mine, trying to get them to *move*. She'd give me a baleful stare and pull on my shoestrings if I happened to walk past empty-handed at feeding time. And if I dared sleep past 6:00 a.m., she'd start thumping at regular, short intervals, then pick up her heavy food crock and bang it on the top platform of her condo.

She'd bite me if I held her too long—and some days, thirty seconds was too long.

Since she continued to progress, we had her spayed and, after healing, paired her with a gentle, neutered bunny. Kumar fell in love with Kali immediately and became her dearest and most comforting friend.

Things were looking up for our darling rabbit.

My father, on the other hand, continued a steady decline. But I found I was better able to assist him now. It was a revelation that Kali was the reason for my new attentiveness. Because of her I was able to think creatively about the care needed in special situations and was applying to my father what I had learned from a rabbit—an affirmation that life is, indeed, mysterious and wondrous.

I traveled back and forth to visit my father, learning valuable lessons from him and from Kali. As he became increasingly weak, she became increasingly strong. I shared stories about her, bringing a smile to his thinning face.

One year and nearly four months after coming to live with us, Kali ran for the first time. Her back legs had to do all the work, but she was fast, her long black skirt flouncing as she made her circuit.

Not long after that, she jumped fourteen inches to the top of a box, then insisted on getting down by herself. Before I could stop her, she did a nosedive, fortunately landing without harm.

She stood on her back legs, a lovely eight inches tall.

It was amazing to watch her. She was so alive! And independent. "Give me liberty!" was her demand whenever I held or groomed her.

Through it all, Kumar was her constant companion. When she'd tire, he'd offer his body as a pillow, cushioning hers for as long as she needed, joining her when she had the energy to romp around the house.

When my father was well enough to be with us for the holidays, he met our rabbits and was immediately enchanted by Kali. From then on, he always asked about her—an endearing memory. It was easier to be lovingly patient with him now, because I had changed.

Kali has been a tremendous catalyst in my life—and a definite blessing. Because of her and the opportunities for learning that she provided, I've glimpsed selfless love, a lofty ideal I thought attainable only in my dreams. I gained a new level of compassion, which helped me to be gentle with my father and with myself. And even though my father is no longer on this earth, I still think of him when I share her stories, remembering his smile as I extol her compelling and valiant spirit.

Kali continues to be a fragile rabbit, but in body only. A model for my life, her attitude and spunk are humbling.

She makes me laugh because she is such a *total* surprise. It wasn't that I had expected a cute, cuddly, sweet little being in the form of a rabbit. I just hadn't expected such power and strength of will. Nor had I realized she'd have such a huge, albeit near silent, voice. Or such *presence*.

Methodically and repeatedly, our beautiful iron-willed maiden has destroyed every notion, every presumption, every wayward thought I ever had about rabbits.

She continues to charge into my quiet midnight times. She never asks if she can come in; she storms, barges, and breaks into my dreams. She *never* tiptoes—I don't think she knows how.

During those night visits, Kali leaps into the heavens, sprinting across the clouds, hopping from star to star— spinning, waltzing, turning, a ballet dancer of purest grace and beauty. I always follow and watch, enthralled. Then, when the moon is full, Kali leaps into the air, carrying my dreams to the heavens and gracing me with bits of wisdom and knowledge as she showers me with stardust.

ABOUT RABBITS: deafness

A rabbit adapts to deafness through the use of other senses and is highly aware of movement, shadow, and vibration. Some vibrations are more easily detected than others, depending on the material transmitting the movement. For example, vibrations coming through a wood floor are easier for a rabbit to sense than those through tile laid on cement. A hearing-impaired rabbit also comes to recognize hand signals and body language and takes cues from the behavior of his humans and other companions.

Care should be taken with activities unfamiliar to the deaf bunny, including bringing something new into the environment, as the disadvantaged rabbit will startle more readily than hearing rabbits and possibly injure himself.

Kali's Prince

Exceptional caregivers embody special qualities, including unconditional love, unending patience, and joyful acceptance. Such attributes are found not only in human helpers but in other animals as well.

This is not a story filled with tension and high drama, but rather an account of stead-fast loyalty and love. It is a tale of dedication, of one small rabbit caring for his disabled mate. This devotion has been his gift to her and an inspiration to us.

I wasn't particularly taken with Kumar the first time I saw him. His mostly-white body with light-gray nose and ears seemed far too plain. I wasn't sure how I felt about his pink eyes either—not that I didn't like pink eyes; I just wasn't sure.

We were at the House Rabbit Society shelter in Broomfield, Colorado—Kumar's rescue-home after he was callously dumped alongside a busy Denver highway.

His eyes begged for consideration. Although I agreed we should adopt him, I harbored the sentiment that he wasn't good enough for our precious little deaf rabbit, Kali. He didn't fit my image of a handsome, elegant rabbit, my choice of companion for our beautiful, black, lop-eared darling.

My husband took a more thoughtful approach. Noting Kumar's sweet temperament, John reminded me that we needed a gentle rabbit to be Kali's friend, one who wasn't too rambunctious for her slight build and fragile constitution.

We'd read about the process of pairing rabbits and how discriminating, or even difficult, some bunnies can be about new friends, so John and I were grateful that someone else would oversee the process for us. If the initial meeting went well, we would leave Kali at the shelter for a few days, until she and Kumar were good friends.

We watched as the two neutered rabbits were put into an area specially set up for pairing. Kali became immediately terrified at the sight of a new rabbit. She stumbled to the gate, frantically beseeching me to take her out of the pen.

I can't leave her in there. She might get hurt. She's scared and needs me. I wanted to pick Kali up and hold her close. I wanted to take her home.

But then I noticed Kumar, who had retreated to the hay box and now sat quietly, munching and watching Kali, waiting for her to relax in his presence. I wondered what he sensed about her.

Give him a chance.

I'd read about the highly social nature of rabbits and felt that having a special friend would benefit Kali. *Give him a chance.* The words competed with my fears.

John and I continued to observe, and within a few hours Kumar had worked his way closer to Kali. A gentle closeness, just enough to let her know she was safe with him. She was definitely cautious, but there was a slight change in her demeanor: she was beginning to relax. We decided to leave her after receiving the promise that the pair would be closely monitored, Kali would not be injured, and we'd be kept apprised of the couple's progress. Trepidation accompanied me home, but I knew Kali was in capable hands.

For the first two days, there was little to report, which made me kind of nervous. But on the third day, the two rabbits were sitting together, eating hay. The next day, Kali let Kumar groom her, and the following evening we happily welcomed them home.

It was immediately obvious that Kumar adored Kali. He groomed her, offered himself as a resting place for her head when she tired of holding herself up, and shielded her body with his whenever he heard an unfamiliar sound.

He was also extravagantly theatrical—his movements so wildly exaggerated that it seemed he would injure himself. We worried something was dreadfully wrong with him, but after careful observation we recognized that he had become intentionally dramatic. Unable to discern the dangerous from the mundane in his new and unfamiliar surroundings, Kumar warned his deaf mate of every potential danger. He'd also amplify his motions when Kali's third eyelids were especially troublesome and prevented clear sight. Or Kumar would thump. Powerful, resonating thumps that alerted Kali—through floor vibrations to her sensitive feet—that something was wrong.

A few days after he came to live with us, the little guy nearly had a heart attack when I brought a laundry basket upstairs. Kumar had seen me ascend and descend the stairs numerous times, but one look at that strange-looking thing in my arms resulted in his taking flying leaps across the floor and into the condo. He bounded to the top platform and, careful not to put his weight on her, placed his body protectively over Kali's.

In that instant I realized what a perfect companion Kumar was. In my mind, he was transformed from a rather plain rabbit to the most incredible, handsome, noble rabbit in the world—the ideal match for Kali. And perfectly named—Kumar, meaning *prince*.

My affection and concern for her now extended also to him. He was reacting to *everything* for Kali's sake, and I wondered how the stress of being constantly on alert would affect him.

To make Kumar's life easier, John and I refrained from unnecessarily alarming our tender-hearted but skittish rabbit. We watched his pink eyes, so marvelously expressive, for signs that he was worried or afraid. "Kumar, it's all right" became our stock phrase, repeated so often that he began looking at us for the reassuring words.

Even though we guarded him against anxiety and distress, he did not have a leisurely life. *I must protect my ladylove and our home* seemed to be his dictum. The sweet, gentle white bunny had his paws full trying to fulfill that promise to Kali, whose frail body belied her strong will. She didn't make it easy for him.

Kali was stalwart, unperturbed in the presence of a stranger working on a window or when a new stray cat took up residence. When we adopted a sweet-tempered dog, whose head was larger than Kali's body, she insisted on crawling over John's legs to greet the part of the prone dog that was at her level—his nose. When I came home on a pair of crutches, Kali disregarded Kumar's warning thumps, hopped over, and took a chunk out of the offensive intruders.

Bill Reed Photography

It took months for Kumar to relax enough to let Kali explore on her own. Even then, his eyes never lost their troubled look until she returned to his side.

Though he remained insecure about Kali's unexpected forays, he actively shared her dislikes. It soon became apparent that a second motto governed his life: *If she likes something, I like it; if she doesn't, neither do I.* When Kali became incensed because I put toys in their condo, Kumar threw them out. I returned them, thinking he might be playing. Kumar then, very deliberately, carried them to the stairs and violently pitched them to the landing below. His message was clear: the toys were *not* to appear in their condo again!

Besides being Kali's protector and champion, he was her teacher, showing her how to drink from a bowl, demonstrating how to properly groom, and sharing the delight of tasting unsweetened papaya treats. When she was not feeling well or was too tired, he'd groom her completely and then offer his body as her bolster.

When Kali became critically ill, Kumar was so distraught that he stopped eating and drinking and quietly lay down beside her, seemingly ready to die with her. We syringe-fed and hydrated him until it became apparent Kali would recover. Then he became exuberant in his joy: running, hopping, spinning, and performing acrobatic feats—enough for both of them.

On days when Kali's body is not working as she would like, or when she is frustrated or angry with something that limits her, Kumar is there: tender and patient, watchful and companionable, with a soft touch and encouraging nudge.

The rabbit who once was a lonely, scared castaway has found his calling: he's Kali's handsome, gracious, and perfect prince.

ABOUT RABBITS: prey animals

Rabbits' actions are greatly influenced by their prey psychology. Everything unfamiliar holds potential danger, making bunnies naturally cautious and distrustful until they verify that conditions are safe. When scared, rabbits may become aggressive in an attempt to defend themselves against perceived perils. Or they can literally become paralyzed with fear or die of fright.

To minimize a rabbit's stress, it's helpful for human guardians to understand what it means to think like a prey animal. Imagine how terrified and stressed you'd be if pursued in a strange environment, unable to find a safe place to hide, and panicked at every unfamiliar movement and sound.

Envision yourself in your rabbit's place, at her eye level. Things that are commonplace to you as a human will take on a different look and meaning, and it will be easier to discern what might frighten her.

LOVABLE BOBKA

Information for this story was provided by Lena Sullivan

It was oppressively hot and bone dry the day someone brought five-month-old Bobka to Bryce Canyon National Park—and left him there.

One can only imagine the young rabbit's fear: no food, no water, nowhere to hide. He was all alone, except for the alarming sounds, unfamiliar odors, and hungry predators.

Domestic rabbits *cannot* survive in the wild. Fortunately for the innocent bunny, campers spotted him and never gave up as he cut back and forth, diving low and jumping high, evading capture until a lucky move snared him. A kind lady contacted Best Friends Animal Society, and the dark-brown bunny was taken to the Utah sanctuary.

There Lena met the lovable rabbit, although he was anything but sweet during their first encounter. It occurred when Bobka was being introduced to another bunny. Staff members hoped the two would become buddies, but Bobka wanted nothing to do with the other rabbit and immediately went on the offensive.

Lena admits she forgot all her training and acted impulsively: in an attempt to stop Bobka's attack, she stuck her hand between the two adversaries. Bobka bit her. *Hard!*

She assumed the bite would not be serious, but Lena soon lost all feeling in two fingers. After a trip to the emergency room and days without full use of her hand, she emerged with a new respect for an angry rabbit. And a clear understanding of why she'd been told never to stick a hand between two fighters.

The next encounter with Bobka was different—he was adorable. His charming and entertaining ways were impossible to ignore, and when Lena later moved back to her home and family in New England, the rabbit who had captured her heart went along.

Bobka treated the cross-country trip as an adventure, settled contentedly into his new life, and finished growing to the size he is today: nineteen pounds of sleek muscle, coupled with a personality that is much, much larger!

Lena delights in recounting some of the intricacies of Bobka's personality.

BOBKA IS INVENTIVE AND CLEVER.

Using his boundless imagination, Bobka often entices Lena to participate in his plans. Like the day he would not come out of his two-story condo.

Worried that he might be ill, Lena opened the doors and knelt on the floor, trying to coax him out. All of a sudden, his big black-brown body vaulted past her head and onto her back!

He dug his toes into Lena's sweatshirt and nudged her neck with his nose. She didn't budge. Bobka prompted again, tickling her cheek with his long funnel ears. Lena crawled across the room, carrying him piggyback all the way to the carpeted area. Once there, Bobka, in one fluid motion, elegantly deposited himself on the floor.

Now, whenever the four-legged jockey wants to be transported in style, he signals Lena by standing up on his hind feet and looking at her with a beatific expression, then putting his forepaws on her legs and bumping his nose against her knee.

Lena generally complies with Bobka's wishes because she loves the reward he so generously bestows: soft kisses with his warm tongue.

BOBKA IS FUN-LOVING AND MISCHIEVOUS.

His favorite furry housemate is Kip, a Pomeranian dog. When Lena adopted Bobka, she was concerned Kip might meddle with the young rabbit. Instead, the two became best friends and often follow in each other's footsteps, checking to see what the other is doing.

When Bobka wants to stir things up, he grabs one of Kip's squeaky toys, then dashes around him, inviting the dog to chase. Kip tries his hardest to keep up with the muscular, long-legged rabbit, but Bobka's air-spins and leaping turns leave the poor dog bewildered.

Kip retaliates by grabbing one of Bobka's favorite chew toys and racing in the opposite direction. A tug-of-war ensues, with low grunts and play growls adding to the theatrics.

When it's all over, the pals snuggle into Kip's bed for a nap.

BOBKA IS SHREWD AND HARD-BARGAINING.

The morning after a long day at the office, Lena always hopes for a few extra minutes of sleep. But as soon as her husband, Casey, opens the rabbit condo, Bobka charges into the bedroom, jumps onto the bed and hops all over her: his way of reminding "mom" to get up and feed him.

Of course, the jolt from his heavy body wakes Lena immediately. She sleepily caresses the dark fur on his mandolin-shaped body, and that's all it takes for Bobka to show his affection—for a second. He licks her cheek with his smooth tongue, then nestles close—and nips her chin! *It's time to feed me!*

He always makes it up to her, though. After eating his portion of pellets and vegetables, Bobka affectionately licks her hand.

BOBKA IS INDEPENDENT AND UNCONVENTIONAL.

He redefines the idea of normal rabbit conduct when he lounges on a cat perch in the window. Lying on his back, all four of his enormous paws dangling above him, Bobka enjoys the sun's warmth on his tummy.

Lena remembers how scared she was the first time she saw Bobka in that position. She quickly walked over to make sure he was breathing and gently felt his side.

Bobka flipped over, glared at her, and thumped his hind feet indignantly. As a clear indication of his displeasure, he turned his back to her before hopping off to find another sunny spot!

BOBKA IS CONFIDENT AND EXUBERANT.

He believes he is King of the House and acts the part. When he's feeling particularly majestic, Bobka pulls the large, ruby-red pillow from Lena and Casey's bedroom to the center of the living room. He settles on top of his throne and defies Kip or the family cat to challenge his sovereignty.

Other times, Bobka performs aerobatics, proclaiming his zest for life. In his unique and infectious rabbit way, he shouts to the world, "*I am having a VERY FINE day!*"

BOBKA IS INTELLIGENT AND IRRESISTIBLE.

As soon as they arrived in New England, Lena instituted a training program and, for the most part, her charming rabbit complied. Litter training was accomplished without a hitch. He always darts to her side when he hears his name, and "Bobka, bedtime" triggers him to run laps around the room, then hop into his house without hesitation.

In other aspects of daily living, however, Lena has had to rely on creativity and consistency because, as all rabbit-people know, rabbits like to be in charge. Bobka is an exceptionally strong-willed bunny; it's a challenge for Lena to keep him mentally stimulated so that he doesn't dig in corners or rearrange furniture.

In his artful fashion, Bobka guides his human companions. When they want to redirect his actions, he redirects theirs. Dragging his dark-blue baby blanket along, he invites them to play his version of hide-and-seek. They loosely turban him in the cotton covering; Bobka nudges his way out, grabs the blanket with his teeth, and races around the room. Then he returns to them, asking for a repeat of the game. And then, a threepeat! He's such a comic that they enjoy playing almost as much as he does.

Bobka is clever, unconventional, entertaining, irresistible, and more: he's one *lovable* rabbit!

ABOUT RABBITS: litter training

In order to be successfully litter-trained with respect to urine, rabbits *must* be spayed or neutered. Rabbits can be taught to deposit most fecal droppings in a box, but will generally leave some dry, easy-to-clean-up droppings as territorial markers. It's easiest to litter-train a bunny after the age of six months, but—like young humans—they sometimes forget and must be gently reminded and assisted in their learning.

Rabbits instinctively avoid relieving themselves in areas where they eat or sleep, which means a rabbit's condo should be roomy enough to accommodate a litter box away from those areas. The box should be large enough to allow the bunny to sit comfortably in it, with sides high enough to prevent urine from streaming over.

Emily

by Susan Chernak McElroy

Her name was Emily, and I don't have a single photo of her anywhere. I do have an ornament in her honor, however. It's a blown-out eggshell that I painted in her image and on the back it reads, *Emily Rabbit*. She came into my life at a blustery time, when the ground around me was uncertain and slippery. I was recuperating from cancer treatments, staying with my boyfriend, wondering where—or if—I would be the coming year.

When in a severe crisis, it has always been my habit to seek out the attention and company of animals. I find myself visiting pet stores and the local humane societies more often when life is storming around me. Sometimes I bring a new animal companion home, unconsciously hoping that a new face in the family will take some of my focus off the hurricanes in my life. It always does. Still, I would not recommend this as a sound strategy for stress reduction and life management. A new animal in the family always comes with surprises of its own. This was certainly true in the case of Emily.

I first began musing about the idea of a house rabbit when I came across the *House Rabbit Handbook* in my local pet store. A house rabbit! What a thought! And so my search began. Mike, my boyfriend, was not opposed to the notion of a rabbit in the house, as he had a special fondness in his heart for bunnies or, that is, for his own personal illusions about bunnies. Culturally, we all share some of these same rabbit fantasies: dreamy notions about the cuddliness of rabbits, their gentleness, their innocence and harmlessness. Rabbits elicit baby talk from humans, and sighs, and all thoughts wonderful and spring-like. When I updated Mike daily on my hunt for the right rabbit, he would smile fondly and his eyes would go all soft.

Down a country road not far from us lived a woman who bred mini lops, and she had a number of baby bunnies all set to go. The one I chose was a tiny female, cinnamon brown with white spots. Only five weeks old, she fit in the palm of my hand and felt as fragile as a newborn chick. We brought her home to a roomy pen set up in the living room, with a sign over it that proclaimed, Rabbit Crossing. Mike was as fussy as a new father, fretting over whether the house was too warm for her, or too cold—or too lonely. He insisted I put a stuffed animal toy in the cage, which she promptly nibbled to shreds and made into a bed. My cat, Sushi, set up a post near Emily's pen, thrilled at this live television show that broadcast nonstop.

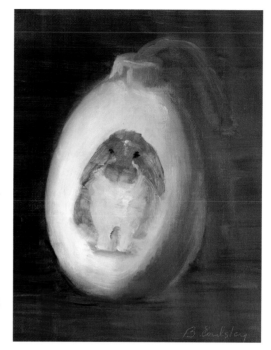

I pulled my scattered attention off the radiation treatments I was having each day, the doctor's appointments I attended each week, and the apprehensions of family and friends (not to mention my own) and placed it on the soothing comfort of Emily's tiny and inquisitive face. Why think of cancer when I could just look at that wiggly nose? Why wonder what turn my little lifeboat would take when I had more pleasing things to worry about, like how to housetrain a baby rabbit and how to create harmony between her and the cat?

Emily settled in easily with us. She was quiet, hungry, curious, and quite brave for her small size. She didn't shrink away when I cupped my hands around her, but she would give a fierce little kick if I did not hold her just right. The litter box in her pen was a source of wonder for her, and she would spend considerable time just sitting in it, reflecting, with her eyes half shut. Sometimes—hallelujah!—she would put it to its intended use. Within two weeks, she was bouncing confidently around the living room while we supervised. I loved it when she raced across the rug and leaped straight up, changing directions high in midair. When she landed after one of those acrobatic feats, she looked downright smug. During Emily's play sessions, Sushi was put into the back bedroom or let outside. In Mike's mind, Sushi did not look at Emily as a potential playmate but as a moving feast. I knew differently. I don't know how I knew, but I just did.

When Mike was at work one day, I introduced cat to rabbit, and they got along instantly and famously. That night when Mike got home, I took Emily out of her pen and confidently placed her on the floor next to Sushi.

Mike was horrified. "Don't do that! Cats are predators!"

As if Mike were a stage director, Sushi suddenly crouched and began stalking Emily as the rabbit bounced across the carpet, oblivious to what lurked behind her.

"Pick her up! The cat's going to eat her!"

I didn't react. They'd been doing this all day.

Emily hopped behind the kitchen counter, Sushi tight on her tail. Mike hollered, "Susan! *DO* something!" In the next instant, Sushi raced out from behind the counter with Emily hot on her tail.

This was the first time Mike had seen the other face of rabbits—the charging bunny, with mouth open and back feet thumping. Emily streaked across the carpet, leaping like a greyhound after Sushi. When she had the cat treed on top of the television, Emily stopped to lick her bunny tail and readjust her nose whiskers. After a final sonorous thump, she calmly hopped to her pen.

This is the nature I came to associate most deeply with Emily. Yes, of course she was sweet and floppy-eared and terminally cute, but I honestly believe her soul was that of a warrior. From her baby-hood, she never suffered fools lightly, myself included. Mike had to adjust his worldview of bunny behavior fast, because after the night she ran Sushi out of the kitchen, Emily pretty much came into her own—and "her own" was the stance of a proud and impatient princess. Sushi was the first to learn of Emily's warrior-princess tendencies, but we would all learn soon enough. Just as Emily was clearly a match for Sushi, in her way she was an equal match for us.

The cat-and-rabbit chase scenes became part of family life, sometimes with Sushi as stalker, sometimes Sushi as prey. Other scenarios were enacted between Emily and me. Sometimes I'd lift her away from chewing on a table leg and she would lie passively in my arms; other times she'd charge my ankles when I tried to distract her from dismantling something I treasured. Her charges were always accompanied by a nasty little growl, and she'd stamp her foot to make her point absolutely certain. If that didn't work, she'd escalate by shaking her ears from side to side while growling and thumping. Mike would never venture near her at moments like this. Any time she got belligerent, her family status changed from *our* rabbit to *my* rabbit.

I never thought of her as cranky. In my eyes, Emily was all the things I wanted to be at that time in my life: strong, self-confident, genuine, direct, honest, sure of personal boundaries. She also had her soft, contemplative side—moments when she delighted in snuggling on my lap or nibbling a grape leaf out in the yard, her eyes all far-away and her jaw munching in a kind of earnest concentration. When she felt like it, she would come when called and race to our feet quick as a flash. She understood "no" and would respect it, but usually accompanied her compliance with a growl. At the time, I was reading books by Dr. Bernie Siegel about cancer survivorship—survivors generally being those who are not docile patients. Emily wasn't docile about anything, but neither was she offensive in her assertiveness. I saw her as a symbol of life—lived with vitality and on one's own terms—and I loved her for it.

Before Emily was a year old, I noticed a funny lump forming on the back of her shoulders, just behind her ears. Our veterinarian recommended surgery and—in accordance with the instructions in my rabbit care books—I asked the vet if she was knowledgeable about the needs of rabbits. She assured me she was, and so I sent Emily off for her surgery with confidence. The operation went fine, the tumor was benign, and I sighed with relief. Emily would not face the kind of exhaustive treatments that had loomed in front of me for so long.

But two days after surgery, things went wrong.

I'd been giving Emily a liquid antibiotic that the vet had assured me was safe for rabbits' delicate digestive systems. It was not. I woke up one morning to a listless bunny covered in murky liquid: her droppings, turned to the consistency of water. Her appetite was gone, her ability to hop gone with it, and she had a horrid, dull look in her eyes. Even her soft fur suddenly felt greasy and smelled sour. I was on the phone to the vet instantly. Emily's health had gone from just-great to critical in thirty-six hours.

The next few days went by in a crazy blur, so reminiscent of my own health fears that I could scarcely breathe into the next moment. Of course, there was medicine to be given my poor, very sick rabbit, along with probiotics to support her digestive system. The hardest treatment for both of us to endure, however, was the insertion of the IV needle under her skin, necessary for the frequent saline drips to keep her hydrated and to avoid kidney failure.

Emily was a good patient. She accepted all my clumsy attempts at nursing with passivity and silence. Forcing medicine and probiotics into her small mouth and piercing her clay-like skin with needles generated no resistance from her. She lay inert on the dining room table—IV bag hanging from the chandelier, tube trailing to her shoulders—staring quietly at nothing.

Suddenly, I understood down to my bones what Dr. Siegel had meant when he wrote that survivors were not necessarily "good" patients. Life should be infused with fervor and spunk, qualities that Emily had seemingly lost. All the traits that made caring for her so *easy*—her listlessness, her quietness, the utter disengagement with her surroundings—felt ominous and deadly. As I tended her, my hands sought vitality and a spark of animation, but found only docility and resignation. And that terrified me.

Time passed, and the days all ran together. Emily was still alive. I swaddled her in terry cloth and diapers between treatments in an attempt to keep her clean and dry. Sometimes when I held her, she would shiver and lick my hand. She was such a good patient—until the moment when she was not.

I had lifted her up to the dining room table for her injection and felt her body tense. She wiggled in my hands.

I tightened my grip, surprised. For a number of days, she'd been hanging from my fingers like a rag. Now, with one hand steadying her, I reached for a needle and popped off the protective cover. She sat quietly until I eased the needle under the skin along her nape. With a grunt, she whirled her head around and glared at me. Then she uttered the sound that made me realize she would be just fine: Emily growled.

Although I'd successfully doctored her by myself for several days, those days were over. I had to wait until Mike came home from work because it now took four hands (preferably five) to give her the medicine and the injections. She wasn't nasty about any of it, just resolute and disgusted and willing to let us know it. Two days later, Emily was charging after Sushi and giving threatening looks at my ankles when I scooted her away from the table legs. So happy was I to see and feel the robust life pouring back into her that I would've been delighted to sacrifice one of my toes to her blustery indignation.

Emily had many more opportunities in her life to be a patient: the tumor returned now and again, one of her teeth came out and the opposing one needed to be trimmed regularly, and she lost a toenail in a mishap. But she was never again a *patient* patient. She was a warrior survivor, and she showed me how to become one as well. I never growled at anyone, nor bit an ankle, but I did become free of cancer. And I send a prayer of remembrance and gratitude to the fierce bunny who taught me how.

ABOUT RABBITS: their true nature

Baby bunnies are definitely adorable, but they do grow up! When they reach adolescence (at approximately 3-1/2 months of age), the once-amiable bunnies begin to display a strong will, a desire for autonomy, and the innate desire to chew and dig.

Not only do rabbits "speak" through a repertoire of sounds and body language, but they may also convey their fears and dislikes by nipping or even biting. Their human guardians should not punish or yell at the bunny for such actions but instead should take the time to learn and appreciate what the bunny is trying to communicate.

As prey animals, rabbits depend on their intelligence and good memories, and they display characteristics (such as being wily and inventive) that make them amusing—and sometimes challenging—companions. They are highly social creatures, which explains the displays of affection and charm for which rabbits are known and loved; it also explains their need for companionship and regular interaction.

Note: Reference the article, "Finding Quality Veterinary Care for Your Rabbit," at the back of this book regarding some of the medications that are toxic to rabbits.

A Real Head-Turner

Information for this story was provided by Patrice Pruitte

He was an unwanted, backyard hutch rabbit. Except for visits by menacing predators and ruffians and by a human who sporadically delivered food and water, the domestic, long-haired bunny lived in solitary confinement. The outdoor hutch was falling in on itself. The rabbit lived in terror, but not for much longer—the predators were making inroads.

A neighbor felt sorry for the little bunny and snuck food to him when she could. She noticed that the child for whom the rabbit had been purchased never played with or cared for him.

Finally, the woman could stand it no longer; her heart filled with mercy, she called a friend, who called her sister. . . .

And that's how I heard about the fuzzy lop who desperately needed a new home.

I didn't want to take him in. Our beloved brown-and-white Dutch rabbit, Chance, was ailing and needed me. But options were nonexistent: as an active volunteer, I knew there wasn't room at The Fund for Animals Rabbit Sanctuary; no one I knew was able to take another rabbit on such short notice; and, if he remained in his current situation, the bunny wouldn't live much longer.

My husband made it easy; he brought the bunny home.

"You won't believe how much fur this rabbit has. Or how matted it is!" Ronnie exclaimed as he entered the house.

I looked inside the small carrier and saw a shaggy animal with a large round head and flat face. Not very rabbit-like, I thought, but cute.

As I watched, the begrimed, tangled mess of a rabbit slowly turned his head from side to side, in a never-ending motion: back and forth, back and forth. The movement was very different from the normal scanning done by rabbits to help reference the objects around them.

"He did that all the way home," Ronnie said in response to my questioning look.

When I reached into the carrier to retrieve our new family member, his fright was obvious: bugged eyes; rapid, almost spastic, breathing; shudders and twitches as if he were on the verge of a seizure.

We carefully placed him in our screened porch, near an open bunny condo. We left the door from the porch to the house open too, so he could roam far and wide, but the frightened little guy immediately chose the security of the condo.

We stayed and watched him settle in. That's when we decided to name him Buffalo because, in profile, his large head, shoulders hunched in stress, and shaggy coat made him look like a diminutive version of his namesake.

Days later, I was fretting about the incessant head-turning, his refusal to come out of his rabbit shelter, the fact that he preferred hiding to eating.

I was also frantic about balancing the care Buffalo needed with all that Chance required.

"It's not that I don't want to spend time with you, but I need to be with Chance too. She's old, and she won't live much longer." My voice cracked as I talked about our precious Dutch rabbit.

It was obvious Buffalo had been psychologically traumatized, but I had no idea how to penetrate his emotional morass. His eyes, the dull deep red of unpolished garnet, had a vacant, unfocused look. I feared the sensitive waif would die.

"Please, help me to help you," I pleaded.

Next thing I knew, I was trying to reason with him, telling him he had to do his part and trust us. My words just tumbled out. I argued against his death; I cajoled, bargained, begged.

The next morning, Buffalo ate all his pellets.

The following afternoon, he came out of his roomy condo. He immediately took up residence out of sight behind a swivel rocker, but I was heartened. It was progress.

"Good for you, sweet boy," I murmured as he snatched a piece of romaine lettuce from my hand.

When Buffalo began exploring the porch, it was with a slow creeping movement, never a hop. Insecure and frightened, he always sought refuge at the slightest sound or movement. Unnaturally cautious and lacking curiosity—he just wasn't *acting* like a rabbit.

Buffalo consistently avoided entering the house. One day we carried him in, and he immediately panicked. We had to return him to the porch, his safe haven. I cradled his sides with my palms and held him on my lap, trying to arrest the violent quakes that seemed to overtake his three-pound body. He crouched down, trying to make himself smaller. His head was turning back and forth, back and forth.

"It's all right, sweet one."

But it wasn't, and I wondered: *Will your emotional scars ever heal? Will you ever be free of your horrible dread?*

I felt I was failing Buffalo, but I didn't know what to do. The head-turning remained a mystery. Perhaps it provided comfort, much like a disturbed child rocking himself. Or maybe the movement was an escape mechanism, a way to shut out the world when it became too scary. No one I spoke with could offer a valid explanation, only that the stress Buffalo had endured the first two years of his life had profoundly affected him. Be patient, they advised.

Sensitive to Buffalo's emotional needs, Ronnie and I spent time with the bunny on his turf. We sat in the screened porch and tried to tempt him with toys, petted him when he'd come within reach, and removed a mat or two from his silky coat whenever possible. I started reading to him from my collection of children's storybooks about rabbits. We gave him time, and more time.

"With love and the right environment, rabbits can overcome adverse beginnings," I kept telling myself.

The holiday season came, a time of mourning the loss of our sweet Chance. Our only decoration was a tiny tree with rabbit ornaments. A vigil light shone through the window onto her fresh grave.

The New Year began on a brighter note. Buffalo began to relax with our handling. We managed to snip off the remainder of the mats and gently loosen tangles; his varicolored Angora coat began to transform into the beautiful covering it was meant to be. After each grooming session, we brought him just inside the door, hoping the close proximity to the porch would allay some of his anxiety. But, alas, he planted his stocky back feet in place and remained motionless, clearly afraid.

Seven months passed. One day Buffalo came to the door and, amazingly, took a step inside the house. He sat there, uncertain, and then retreated. But it was a breakthrough.

Then, on a particularly cold morning in May, I closed the door to the porch, only to hear scratching a few minutes later.

I opened the door, in time to see Buffalo dash into hiding. I left it open, and our fuzzy lop ventured in! Not very far, not for very long, but he came into the house on his own. My hopes soared.

Ronnie and I marked time by Buffalo's forays into the unknown. Fourteen months after coming to our house, he took a short nap on the plush carpet in the living room.

On the anniversary of Chance's death, Buffalo slept in the den, closer to our bedroom. A week later, he started running and hopping! Then, miraculously, the head-turning behavior disappeared.

That Christmas, the unfamiliar sight of our large evergreen tree sent Buffalo back into the grip of terror. We held him and loved him, but for two weeks the porch was his asylum.

The morning Buffalo rejoined us, he raced past the tree and into the den. He peeked around the door and then courageously positioned himself to watch the towering, needle-leafed intruder. Later that day, searching for him, I discovered Buffalo soundly asleep—under the Christmas tree!

I laughed and I cried. Our little Buffalo was healing.

Then came a day I'll always remember: Valentine's Day, and Buffalo sought *me* out. His intense garnet-colored eyes, clear and sparkling with mischief, said, "Play with me!" And that wasn't all; he actually began asking Ronnie for back rubs.

Buffalo was transforming, day by day. He eagerly explored the house, hid under beds and in cardboard boxes, and discovered the versatility of phone books. Exhibiting the wonderful disposition of a happy rabbit, he saw everything as an adventure.

Today Buffalo is a gorgeous rabbit. When he moves, his fur is an undulating wave of beige, misty gray, and white. If lying in repose, his white throat and belly shimmer in the light. He hops, and his dark gray ears flop in graceful rhythm. When asking for a treat, he displays delicate front paws—one white, one gray.

It took more than two years, but Buffalo finally knows he is safe and in his forever home. Now, he runs to greet us, his eyes bright and knowing, and we see a rabbit who comprehends love. He runs to greet others and always receives a second glance, and a third. Buffalo is so handsome, and he exudes such happiness and personality. The once traumatized and fearful rabbit is a beautiful example of confidence, sweetness, and charm—he's become a *real* head-turner!

ABOUT RABBITS: backyard hutches

Rabbits who live in outdoor hutches receive virtually no mental stimulation and little protection. Predators are able to access many hutches, chewing or tearing them apart. Even if an enclosure is inaccessible, the mere presence of a predator can cause a rabbit to panic and injure herself or to go into shock and die.

Most hutches provide limited refuge from wind, freezing temperatures, heat, rain, and snow. In addition, nearly all hutches are too small and most have wire floors—a combination that leads to obesity, weak muscles, deformed spines, damaged feet, and other health problems. Poor husbandry and the lack of adequate health care result in many preventable maladies.

The fact that backyard hutch rabbits generally live alone and receive limited human interaction prevents their lively and intricate natures from developing fully. Domestic rabbits are the third most popular mammalian pet, underscoring their initial appeal as companions. But they are also the most likely to be abandoned or taken to an animal shelter (where they are likely to be euthanized).

Humans must be emotionally involved with their rabbits in order to have happy, healthy pets—and backyard hutch rabbits are too often denied that emotional commitment.

A Perfect Gent and Lady Defiance

Information for this story was provided by Valerie Fox

Bailey? Well, she's a gorgeous bunny filled with sweetness and sass. She's gregarious, brazen, and bold." I sounded unabashedly proud. "She's my baby."

My friend Marie grinned as I began pulling photos of the beautiful mini lop from my wallet. She marveled at Bailey's coloring—caramel tan accented with dark ash—and remarked on her soulful gaze. Appreciating Marie's intent interest, I continued talking.

"Bailey is really independent, but when she wants attention, she'll run around our feet and stand on her hind legs to be picked up. Or if I sit down, she runs over and rests her head on my ankle while I pet her."

Then I wondered, "Why did you ask about her?"

As I listened, the smile faded from my face. Marie was suggesting that her foster rabbit might be the perfect companion for Bailey.

"Oh, I don't know," I mumbled.

Seeing through my hesitation, she said, "You know, a single rabbit is often bored and lonely, and a bored bunny can be really destructive."

But still I hemmed and hawed, and the subject was dropped.

When I mentioned a second rabbit to my husband, Dave, he shuddered. Don't get me wrong, he thinks Bailey is wonderful; he's the one who knew I wanted a bunny and adopted her for me. But Bailey had only one fault, and it was one we did not appreciate. She loved to chew. No matter what we did, our bunny-proofing efforts were ineffectual. We wondered if she was being incorrigible or if other rabbits were just like her. Bailey was a handful. Two rabbits? What if the other bunny was like her? I shuddered too.

However, the seed was planted. Dave and I discussed the possibility of adopting a companion for Bailey. But we'd just purchased our first house, so we also talked about the potential

Valerie Fox

damage to our lovely new home. Were we being selfish? And was our concern valid: would two rabbits wreak double havoc?

Not more than a week later, Dave heard an interview on the radio. Calling me from work, his first words were, "We've got to get Bailey a bunny buddy." He followed with a discourse on the social nature of rabbits and how lonely and depressed they become when their human companions are gone all day.

This new information helped us realize that Bailey's great excitement when we returned home each day was actually a symptom of her loneliness. That did it. I called Marie; the bunny was still available for adoption. I visited and fell in love with the handsome, upright-eared rabbit. The name Baron suited him: he was a gentleman with noble bearing, clothed in a luscious coat of dark charcoal with black swirls, distinguished by a white nose and white-tipped toes.

Marie and I agreed that the pairing of Bailey and Baron would take place in the foster home's small, cozy bathroom, neutral territory for both rabbits. The day arrived for me to deliver Bailey, and my concerns for our little girl were numerous. *What if she got hurt? What if the stress made her sick? What if my baby liked Baron so much that she ignored me? What if. . . ? What if. . . ?* I was nervous, more nervous than Bailey.

The setting for the first day was perfect: two side-by-side cages so Baron and Bailey could slowly get used to each other. They didn't seem too concerned about each other's presence, which made me feel hopeful.

The next day, I returned to Marie's, arriving mid-morning when the rabbits were in their lazy mode. I stood at the baby gate, looking for Bailey. A box moved and out poked her head. Baron was on the opposite side of the bathroom, eating hay from one of the bins. I stayed to supervise and intervene if necessary, but not much seemed to be happening. They groomed themselves, looked disinterested, took a nap.

Two hours later, Baron made his move. He cautiously approached Bailey and got close enough so he could stretch forward and touch her nose with his. No sooner did his neck begin to extend than Bailey went into action.

She stood on her hind legs. *SLAP!* Bailey brought her front paws down on Baron's nose. Then she snorted and grunted. I couldn't believe it: my five-pound angel-face sounded downright crude!

Baron retreated, rubbed his nose with his paws, then tried again. Bailey slapped him as before. Baron hopped back to his side of the bathroom, cleaned his sweet face, and hunkered down, pretending not to care.

After dinner, Baron made a roundabout entry into Bailey's space. This time, my little spitfire thwacked him hard and followed up with a nip.

It was obvious Baron had never met such a defiant female! He didn't know what to do, how to act. I found myself wishing Bailey was a bit more genteel, more a lady.

Valerie Fox

Two days passed. Bailey wouldn't give an inch. I'd never seen rabbits paired before but, tickled though I was with her spunk, it seemed to me that Bailey was being somewhat ungracious and bad-mannered. Baron, on the other hand, continued to be patient, polite, and thoughtful.

To give the pairing process a little nudge, Marie suggested we take the two rabbits for a car ride, as sharing such an uncomfortable experience distracts rabbits from their usual patterns and often helps them bond. I rejected the idea, afraid of stressing Bailey. But, next thing I knew, Marie was handing me a carrier and asking for my assistance in getting both rabbits into it.

Interpreting my horrified look correctly, she hastened to allay my fears. "I've done this often enough to know these two are not going to harm one another; they're going to be great friends."

After guiding Baron and Bailey into the carrier, Marie put it into my arms and told me to walk around the house, simulating a car ride. I did, feeling just a bit foolish, but soon found myself making a few engine noises and enjoying the excursion.

That unsettling event caused a noticeable change in Bailey. Out of the carrier and every bit the complicated female, she now acted the coquette and enticed Baron to chase her. Desperate for a friend, he willingly did his part. She'd stop sometimes and turn around. He'd get close, hoping for a friendly exchange, and she'd bat his nose! Baron would wiggle and shake his ears, trying to make sense of her actions. But the two made some kind of breakthrough because the next morning they were eating hay from the same bin and sharing a litter box.

After that it was easier for Baron, but not all rosy. Off and on, Bailey kept exhibiting her coarse behaviors. When Baron finally had his fill of her moods, he roared in rabbit-speak, *ENOUGH*, by biting her. Assertiveness must have felt good because, from then on, Baron began fighting back. And Bailey began settling down.

I was pleased by their progress because our house was empty without Bailey. Rabbits may seem quiet, but they have a huge presence. After seven lonesome days, I was happy to bring the couple home.

It took quite a while for Baron to feel comfortable in his new digs. He'd endured a tough early life, cast out to die by an uncaring person. Fortunately he had been found and taken to Brambley Hedge Rabbit Rescue in Phoenix where my friend, Marie—one of their foster parents—came to know him. Now he was home with us, getting used to strange sounds, our schedules, and a new "sister," our golden retriever. Though timid at first, adjust he did.

Baron continues to be a perfect gent, and I'm happy to say that Bailey has acquired some of his cultivated traits and is more a lady now. They snuggle on the grass mat, groom each other, play and leap about the living room, race up and down the stairs, and run to us for lovin'. They are a perfect pair.

Oh, and Bailey no longer has a hankering to chew baseboards and other delectables. Now she's got better things to do.

ABOUT RABBITS: making friends

Rabbits can be very picky about their choice of companions. Some become friends quickly, while others require months to become close. Putting two rabbits together and expecting them to immediately like each other is unrealistic and unfair. Hostility between rabbits (especially if either is unaltered) may result in serious, life-threatening fights.

Though domestic rabbits are communal creatures, the successful pairing of two or more bunnies requires care, time, patience, and a neutral space. When the friendship is cemented, it's a wonderful feeling to know that two convivial fur-friends have each other for comfort and comradeship while family members engage in work, school, and other activities. An added benefit is that a companion reduces boredom and the related destructive chewing. Finally, it's a pleasure to be welcomed home by two happy bunnies—and watching their antics provides delightful entertainment!

The Tilted Butterfly

Information for this story was provided by Stephen Guida

My heart fractured around the edges as I stared at her: a gnarled ball of tan-and-white fur, patched with bare skin raw from urine burn. And her head was all wrong. Fixed at a 90-degree angle, it lay sideways and parallel to the padded-cage floor. Only one eye was visible; wide with apprehension, it pointed toward the ceiling.

Pity, anger, and powerlessness replaced my confidence. I barely heard a voice recounting the recent events: originally called in on a case of dog abuse, authorities had found the injured rabbit in a tiny, filthy wire cage in the backyard. Rescued along with the canines, she'd been taken to Brambley Hedge Rabbit Rescue.

Estimated to be six months old, the lop-eared bunny had been the victim of violence. A veterinarian diagnosed neurological damage due to neck injury and perhaps permanent damage to her inner ear. The result: a severe impairment and lack of balance that destined her to a tilted view of the world.

A sudden movement startled the defenseless rabbit. Her eye filled with dread; she flinched in fear and began to panic.

And then it happened.

Losing her balance, she pitched to her side. Kicking desperately in an attempt to return to a sitting position, her frail body slammed into the walls of the padded cage. She began rolling uncontrollably; her head bobbled as it followed the fast rotation of her body, spinning, twisting, whirling.

It seemed forever before comforting hands held the rabbit upright, but the entire incident had taken just seconds.

The dizziness passed and the bunny's rapid breathing slowed. She stilled, and her dark eye once more aimed skyward.

My heart sank as the full extent of her condition became apparent. Although I had agreed to be her foster-parent, I had never cared for a disabled bunny before. Questions raced through my mind: *Will you have to spend the rest of your life inside a padded cage? How will I keep you safe? Will you ever get better? What can I possibly do to help you gain some semblance of a normal life?*

Stephen Guida

Then Baby Girl, as I had already named her, shifted her head just slightly and her coffee-colored eye interrupted my thoughts. Can I trust you?

I slowly reached forward. Baby Girl allowed me to stroke her soft fur, calming further under my touch.

I'll never harm you.

Despite those true words, my concerns remained. I was afraid for her, afraid of my ignorance.

To manage those fears, I learned how to meet her most immediate needs—feeding, cleaning, and picking her up. At my first attempt, I failed to hold her properly and Baby Girl became frantic in her insecurity. I became equally frantic as she nearly squirmed out of my arms in an effort to find something solid beneath her feet.

When I finally got the knack of lifting and holding her, she trustingly leaned her worn body against me. What a thrill that was. I remember feeling Baby Girl's heart racing and thumping. Or was it mine?

I took her home, and my days developed a gentle rhythm as I became Baby Girl's parent, nurse, waiter, and guardian. I performed every routine task necessary for keeping my disabled charge fed, clean, medicated, dry, safe.

Without complaint, Baby Girl allowed me to care for her and willingly took her medications. I gently massaged her body, hoping to perhaps reverse some of the damage to her neck. In response, she'd blissfully relax and move her jaws rapidly back and forth, making a soft purring sound with her teeth. To give Baby Girl something different to look at, I began carrying her from window to window so she could see the world beyond the house—she seemed to love this, and so did I.

Baby Girl was so helpless and prone to "episodes" that I moved my home office into the living room where she was. I became nearly compulsive in my efforts to do things quietly, to refrain from any fast or unfamiliar movements that might trigger a thrashing, tumbling scare.

I made mistakes, like the day I unloaded supplies in the living room. Since Baby Girl had seen the boxes, I didn't think twice when the time came to move them into the garage.

I lifted a large box. Baby Girl panicked as her skyward-looking eye spied the dark, unfamiliar form suddenly appearing in her field of vision. She teetered, flipped over, and tumbled around and around until I could open her cage and stop her.

Finally my terrified foster bunny was in my arms. Eyes bulging, heart racing, lungs sucking air, she cuddled into me and gradually relaxed as her dizziness subsided.

I'm so sorry. So very sorry. The words were an incessant parade in my mind.

She stirred and her dark eye interrupted my thoughts. I trust you.

Everything stilled. Awareness flowed through me: Baby Girl was an extraordinary gift—and she'd been given to me.

She shouldn't be captive in a cage; she deserved better than that. When I felt she'd gained enough strength, Baby Girl enjoyed daily time in a playpen; gradually, she began inching slowly around it.

One spring day, I decided she was ready for something new and cleared a space in the living room. The vernal equinox was just days away and it was unseasonably warm; "Spring" from Vivaldi's *Four Seasons* graced the air, befitting the occasion.

I reached into Baby Girl's cage and picked her up, carefully supporting her backside with one hand, nestling her front paws and head against me with the other.

Our usual morning meander was shortened by my impatience. A stop at one window allowed her to see the goings-on outside, and then. . . .

I carefully positioned Baby Girl on the living room carpet.

Making sure all four feet were square beneath her, my hands cradled her in place. Doubts began their harassment: *What if she loses her balance and starts spinning? What if she gets hurt?* Now that the time had come, I was loath to let go.

But Baby Girl was ready and nipped my finger to show her impatience!

Time to let go.

She excitedly looked around, her "up" eye scanning the room, her "down" eye focused on the floor. She took a couple of tentative test-steps. For thirty seconds she was in a new world. Then she slipped.

My heart slammed into my ribs. I wouldn't get to her fast enough.

Baby Girl flipped over onto her side, but instead of spinning out of control, she did a complete barrel-roll and righted herself. She regained her footing! On her own!

Utter relief flooded me. Elation surged through my veins. My chest buoyed with pride: I was like the father who saw his child take her first steps.

With wonder and excitement, mixed with a huge dose of trepidation, I watched Baby Girl take baby-step after baby-step. My heart seemed to fail each time she lost balance, then started beating again when she regained her foothold.

In an effort to calm myself, I pulled the morning newspaper to the floor. I glanced at a headline, peeked at Baby Girl, skimmed a phrase, and gave it up. I couldn't read; my only interest was this bit of bunny making her own history.

She wobbled back to me and stared me in the face, then nudged me with her white nose as if to say, *Well, how about THAT!*

I couldn't resist. I pulled her close and hugged her, my little special-needs bunny who was working so hard. Explaining that she'd exercised her weak body enough for one day, I gathered her up, and we resumed our daily amble about the house.

When we stopped at Baby Girl's favorite window, monarch butterflies—those amazingly beautiful messengers of spring—fluttered about the orange trumpet-shaped flowers of the Cape May honeysuckle bushes. The sight of them capped an already perfect morning.

After that red-letter spring day, Baby Girl began roaming free when the other rabbits were in their condos.

She graduated to a slow, careful walk.

Months passed. She began scampering across the carpet. Then darting.

Not long after that, another banner day: Baby Girl ran! Admittedly it was a kind of lopsided effort as she ran in a right-turn circle, the only direction her head-tilt allowed. Then she took a flying leap of faith and landed true on her feet inside the litter box! *MY* head-tilt bunny performed a feat not normally attempted by one with such fragile balance. Her exit was not as graceful, but she made it.

Wow! Baby Girl!

That night the padded cage took up permanent residence in the garage, and Baby Girl gained her own rabbit condo.

A confident, sparkly-eyed Baby Girl began asserting herself, zigzagging swiftly away when she didn't want to be picked up. She greeted each day with gusto and enthusiasm; I marveled at her transformation.

Spring came 'round again, and it was time for another new experience. I decided to let Baby Girl meet Cisco, a large, handsome satin-mix who was my unfailing "nurse bunny."

Cisco bounded over to Baby Girl. She stopped dead in her tracks, her amazement at this living, breathing, bouncing ball of black fur almost palpable.

Cisco bowed his head to the floor, asking to be groomed. Baby Girl would do no such thing! She joyfully ran all around him, nudging and

Stephen Guida

sniffing, then shoved *her* head underneath his, insisting he groom her instead. Gentle soul that he is, Cisco initiated grooming, and the two of them happily exchanged affection.

When she tired, Baby Girl draped herself over Cisco's recumbent body, using him as a big warm pillow. He recognized she was special and seemed to enjoy supporting her delicate body.

Later that morning, Baby Girl and I took our daily stroll through the house. Vivaldi's masterpiece was a murmur in the background as I walked to the window so she could view her favorite honeysuckle bush. My heralds of spring were back: large monarchs decorated the flowered shrub with their gorgeous orange-and-black wings.

One of the beauties sailed toward the honeysuckle, its wings held in a V. I wanted to see it through Baby Girl's eyes and mimicked her head position.

The butterfly tilted. I saw the delicate tremors of the lacy wing, the tan underside, the sun's rays piercing the shimmering black veins and tiny white spots in the black borders. I was seeing what Baby Girl saw. We were experiencing together the exquisite beauty of the monarch, the pure simplicity of the moment.

And then it happened.

My notions about Baby Girl being different, about her being a disabled bunny, took wing and floated away. Everything seemed to spin around the awareness that Baby Girl was a normal bunny.

My perceptions, my definitions, my labels—they had precluded me from seeing her as she really was. Oh, sure, I rarely noticed the head tilt anymore, but Baby Girl had always been my "special needs" bunny.

Now I knew better. But she hadn't changed, *I had.*

I get it. BABY GIRL, I GET IT!

Her self-possessed nature shone through her bright eye as she steadily looked into mine.

Yes. Given enough time, I knew you would.

ABOUT RABBITS: a bunny's body—and handling

A rabbit's body is composed of a well-developed musculature, especially in the hindquarters. The rabbit's muscles encompass a disproportionately greater mass than the delicate skeleton. This muscle-to-bone ratio underscores the necessity for exercise and playtime. Confinement and lack of exercise result in frail bones (osteoporosis) and weak muscles, which make the rabbit susceptible to injuries, some of them life-threatening.

Injuries also result from improper handling and can include fracture of the vertebrae and damage to the bunny's spinal cord. Being dropped or forced to jump from too high a place is likely to damage legs and leg joints. The number of rabbits injured and disabled by improper handling is one of the reasons rabbit-knowledgeable people declare that bunnies are not good pets for children.

FRANKIE'S FOIBLE

by Nancy LaRoche
Information for this story was provided by Bea LeNoir

The black-and-white rabbit crouched in a carrier on the seat of the patrol car, ears pricked forward as the patrolwoman and a gruff voice talked on the two-way radio.

"I have an injured domestic rabbit that needs a vet," the policewoman said into the microphone.

"I don't give a damn about any old rabbit," the voice interrupted. "Take it to Animal Control."

"Sir, I think vet care—"

"I said, ANIMAL CONTROL."

The loud, unfriendly tone scared the rabbit. He tucked in on himself, getting as small as he could, pressing his ears flat against his shoulders.

"Yes, sir," the woman answered quietly, clicking off her microphone.

Then, speaking to her furry passenger, she said, "Animal Control doesn't have much space right now, and I couldn't stand it if you were killed. Don't worry, little bunny. I've got a plan."

The patrol car followed the beam of its headlights through darkened neighborhoods and into the outskirts of the Colorado town. The six-month-old bunny tensed when the vehicle stopped.

His crate was lifted and suddenly the rabbit was in. . . a chicken coop! His ears swiveled and his sensitive nose wiggled as he took in the unfamiliar sounds and smells.

"I'm guessing you aren't going to be too pleased with this arrangement," the woman told him. "But it's the best I can do tonight."

She cleaned and blocked off one corner of the coop, put hay and a bowl of fresh water down on the floor, and then let the rabbit out of the carrier.

"I don't think you'll get sick from just one night with the chickens," she whispered as she petted his nose. "I'll see you in the morning."

Hours later, as the light of dawn began seeping into the chicken house, his new friend returned. "The House Rabbit Society folks are going to take care of you, little one," she said happily.

The car ride didn't seem so fearful this time; he trusted the human who chauffeured him to the Denver metro area. A lady named Bea was waiting for them. The rabbit relaxed as he listened to the friendly voices.

Bea opened the carrier and scooped him up. "Oh! Poor baby!" she exclaimed. "Look at the mangled flesh on his neck and face. And his eye—he can't close it. What happened to him?"

"I don't know, Bea," the officer replied glumly. "I found him cowering at the side of a road."

"I'll get him to my vet right away."

The patrolwoman petted the bunny one last time. He licked her fingers in thanks, then willingly let Bea put him in a carrier.

"Your name will be Frankie," she told him as they started the drive.

Within an hour, Frankie was in the hands of Bea's trusted vet. After thoroughly examining the rabbit, he shook his head, then said solemnly, "Someone put a rope around this rabbit's neck and swung him around. Abscesses have developed in the rope-burn wounds. The injuries have stretched the skin on his face, which is why the eyelid isn't working."

Frankie's extensive injuries required surgery that day. The abscesses were cleaned and the skewed eyelid fixed so that it would shut. By the time Bea picked Frankie up that evening, his nails were trimmed and fur combed. He looked wonderful, in spite of the sores circling his neck and marring his face.

When Bea put Frankie into the room prepared for him, he knew he was safe. He began kissing her face, licking her with love and gratitude. She laughed with delight as the soft, barely damp tongue groomed every part of her that was within reach.

Frankie turned out to be the perfect houseguest—his behavior was so impeccable that he was soon allowed to roam at will. His favorite activity was to follow his new best friend everywhere, even when it required jumping three-foot baby gates!

It was only when Bea remained stationary for a time that Frankie dashed off to explore every nook and cranny he could find. He ignored the soreness of his face and neck and turned every room into a dance parlor, dashing, leaping, and springing into the air to kick sideways or to spin around. He seemed to be saying, "Forget the *bad* people;

I'm with *good* people. Everything is wonderful! *REJOICE!*" His positive outlook bounced through the house with him.

But when Bea called his name, he rushed to her, eager to be picked up and cuddled. He was content to sit on her lap for hours at a time, alternately tooth purring and grooming her. In return for his presence, he *demanded* that she pet him. Bea always smiled at him and teased, "You have a weakness for love!"

One cold November day, the five-pound bunny was healed enough to be taken on a very special excursion—to the television studio of the local NBC affiliate.

Frankie was one of several adoptable rabbits Bea wished to showcase. Seconds before the cameras rolled, she handed him to the anchorman conducting the interview. Frankie was happy to receive gentle caresses and sat sedately in place, eliciting comments about his charming personality.

When the segment ended, the newsman made the "mistake" of reaching to shake hands with Bea instead of continuing to pet Frankie. In the flash of an eye, the rabbit nipped his arm, telling the man in no uncertain terms that he expected to be petted *nonstop*. Startled, the poor fellow leapt to his feet, dumping Frankie into Bea's arms.

Bea wasn't sure who was more surprised, she or the anchorman. *Thank goodness we're off camera*, was her first thought.

She conveyed both apology and humor as she quickly explained Frankie's need for affection. She was relieved when the newsman laughingly forgave Frankie and labeled his penchant for petting as "Frankie's foible."

Frankie's public appearance generated viewer interest. As much as Bea loved his company, she was happy when a family chose him and three other rabbits for adoption. She helped introduce the four bunnies to one another, and a few days later the group was ensconced in their own room, in their new forever home.

Now Frankie thinks he's in heaven: he has human *and* bunny friends to give him love and attention. His penchant for petting

hasn't changed one bit. When he craves human contact, he runs up and nudges an ankle. After someone caters to his request, Frankie lavishly bestows bunny kisses. It's his way of happily admitting, "I have a weakness for love!"

ABOUT RABBITS: creating a trusted friendship

Some rabbits love to be held and petted; they'll sit on their human's lap, tooth-purring in contentment. Other rabbits may prefer to receive petting and affection while seated next to their human on the floor. Still others seem to hate being held or fondled and may scrabble to get away.

Becoming a bunny's trusted friend requires time and effort and the awareness of what it means to be a prey animal. The amount of socialization bunnies receive when young influences their reactions to humans. Rabbits are less stressed when they are familiar with family activities and when their condos are respected as private spaces.

When rabbits run away from someone or prepare to defend themselves, it's because they do not trust that person. In human-rabbit relationships, humans must not only *be* trustworthy, but must also convince the rabbits that they *are* trustworthy.

Regardless of how much he or she may enjoy your company, do not expect your bunny to love attention as much as Frankie. Few rabbits will come when called and many do not "kiss." It's important to respect each rabbit's uniqueness and to never expect a bunny to act like an affectionate dog.

Interiors by Taz

Information for this story was provided by Elisha Bunting

Elisha was smitten the first time she saw the light-gray, pug-nosed Holland lop.

Her feelings were not returned.

Elisha offered the back of her hand for the new arrival to sniff.

Taz, his name according to the cage tag, transformed from a cute little bunny into a menacing attacker. Tail up and body tense, he lunged at her. Harsh snorts and flattened ears warned her away.

Elisha immediately backed up but was unfazed. She knew the small rabbit was just trying to defend himself and that he probably had good reason.

"What's his story?" she asked.

"He arrived from the clinic an hour ago," her co-worker replied, referring to the veterinary clinic where animals are taken upon arrival at Best Friends Animal Society. "He came from an elementary school."

That explained much. Elisha knew that most school classrooms are unsuitable for rabbits: the social animals too often exist in small cages, without regular exercise or adequate stimulation for their inquisitive minds. In addition, children—in their eagerness to interact with the animals—often poke objects into the cage, creating a fearful and defensive rabbit. It was likely that whoever had previously been responsible for Taz didn't understand his nature or his needs.

She peered at the lop, now immobile and flattened to the floor of his cage, as though trying to vanish from sight.

"He puts up a defense when someone gets too close, but this little guy is absolutely petrified," Elisha observed.

A look of determination fixed on her face. She would help him learn to trust again, step by step. The first phase: tidying his cage. She opened it and, as she anticipated, the terrified bunny launched himself at her.

Using a towel as a barrier against the agitated rabbit, in record time a clean litter box and heavy water bowl were in place, the door latched.

A furious Taz reacted to Elisha's encroachment: he shredded the towel that cushioned the cage floor, flung hay about, scratched food pellets into the clutter. He studied his work and, apparently not satisfied with the mess he'd created, began pushing against the water crock. It tilted, then emptied.

Half-smiling as she watched the zealous rabbit express his anger, Elisha shook her head in disbelief when the three-pound lop, small enough to easily sit on top of a paperback book, pulled the full-sized litter box to the center of the cage, got his head under it, and tip. . .*tip*. . .*TIPPED* it over.

In less than ten minutes: a shambles!

Elisha wasn't about to let the fast-acting bohemian sit on the damp floor; she duplicated her earlier actions, this time fastening a water bottle after removing the bowl.

The daily pattern was established. Taz became a raging, destructive fiend whenever Elisha dared intrude into his home. In turn, Elisha visibly brightened whenever she looked at the bushy-banged lop. She thought everything about him—expression, actions, and attitude—was adorable.

Learning more about Taz's early history shed light on his behavior. While in the school classroom, he'd lived with another rabbit. The two neutered bunnies were bonded companions; they comforted and loved one another. One weekend they were left without adequate food and water. Taz somehow survived; his best friend did not. After that tragic event, Taz was given to one of the children, whose mother immediately noted medical problems. Not knowing how to properly care for a rabbit, she made arrangements with Best Friends and drove Taz from Arizona to the sanctuary in Utah.

At his new home, Taz sometimes vented his rage, distrust, and frustration on everyone and everything. Other times he acted so withdrawn and despondent over the loss of his dearest rabbit friend that staff members worried about his will to survive.

Elisha concentrated on befriending Taz and finding ways to pique his interest. It was a relief when, after eleven days at the Bunny House, he began showing interest in his surroundings, a sign the small lop was ready for something new.

Elisha carried his cage to an empty outdoor play area, quickly opened his door, then stepped out of the enclosure. Taz charged out, spun and looked around. Satisfied he was alone, he crouched down, using his superior hearing and smell to inspect the unfamiliar setting.

Abruptly, he jumped straight into the air. Dark eyes sparkling, Taz hopped, leaped, kicked, side-jumped. His lop ears flopped in rhythmic tempo; his movements caused the coral-hued sand to pattern around him. Taz seemed a bunny without a care in the world.

Elisha Bunting

As suddenly as the frolic began, it ended. Taz sat quietly cleaning himself and then repeated the entire routine again. And again.

Elisha, jubilant to see "her" rabbit so happy, stepped inside the enclosure to play with Taz—and met his furious alter ego. Ears leveled, mouth open, he barreled forward, a rumbling growl in his throat.

Elisha refused to be upset. As she herded the young rabbit into his cage, she confidently promised him that some day soon he'd trust her. But as soon as the door closed, Taz's eyes turned dull; his head slumped dejectedly to the floor—he hated being confined. The dramatic change in his demeanor affected the normally composed Elisha. She began crying, recognizing that Taz, in his rabbit way, was weeping too.

Weeks turned into months. One sunny autumn day, Elisha succeeded in becoming the first person to groom Taz without being bitten. The "little monster" turned into her "sweet cuddlebunn." He even began grooming himself while sitting on her lap. What an amusing contrast: the "messiest rabbit ever" was singularly meticulous in his personal habits.

The New Year arrived. Elisha introduced Taz to Chaunta, rescued by a good-hearted man watering his rosebushes. The abandoned rabbit, just eight weeks old at the time, had been nearly invisible as she crouched among the thorny plants. Persistence paid off, and she was captured and taken to Best Friends.

At first, Chaunta was very displeased with the partner Elisha selected for her and launched into a tiff. Taz responded in like manner. Elisha supervised, blithely certain the strong-tempered rabbits would work out their dominance issues. They did.

Now two beautiful lop-eared rabbits—the dove-gray Taz and the charcoal-colored Chaunta—share a room specially built just for them. Taz continues to exhibit his peculiar, disheveled decorating style, while Chaunta specializes in rearranging furniture. Her favorite activity is running to other parts of the bunny-proofed house and nosing around, to her liking, items large and small. Taz willingly follows his partner everywhere and acts as her assistant.

And who lovingly watches over them? Elisha, of course. She adopted the pair and delights in seeing them exhibit the full range of their personalities. Taz frequently shows his appreciation and affection by crawling onto her lap and licking her hand before dashing off to rejoin his honeybunn.

Taz and Chaunta: the two glory in their freedom, in the joy of turning everything into something fun. With Elisha's tolerant understanding and care, theirs is a world of possibilities!

ABOUT RABBITS: when a bunny's furred friend dies

When a rabbit loses a partner, it's very important he be allowed to reconcile himself to the friend's death. The bunny should be permitted to remain with the dead body in the privacy of the rabbits' home, where he may groom the body, snuggle with it, or even drag it around, trying to get his best friend to "wake up." It may take several hours, but eventually the bunny will move away from the body, realizing that his partner is gone.

If a rabbit isn't given the opportunity to come to terms with his partner's death—if the friend just disappears—he'll be bewildered, anxious, heartbroken, and perhaps angry. He may sink into a deep depression, sometimes refusing to eat or drink. Like humans and other animals, rabbits need closure when their best friends die.

A rabbit who is permitted to come to terms with his companion's death will go through a period of grieving, usually lasting two or three weeks. He will seem to be a little "down," but generally won't be so deeply depressed that he quits eating or drinking. Spend extra time with him and share his grief—he'll understand that you're hurting too. Occasionally, the bunny will need to complete the grieving process before he is comfortable meeting another potential rabbit partner. But it's not unusual for a bunny who has accepted his companion's death to break out of the grieving pattern when appropriately introduced to a new and compatible pal.

A Treasure Found

Information for this story was provided by Caroline Gilbert

November in Hilton Head, South Carolina, was a perfect time
to be in the coastal resort community: the humidity was lower,
most of the tourists were gone, hurricane season was coming
to an end. Life on the island was returning to normal.
Except for one small bunny.

Paralyzed with fear, he hunched next to a cardboard box that had fallen from the
dumpster.

Someone had taken him to the forsaken place and left him there.

Alone.

With neither food nor water.

His long ears registered danger and he flattened himself against the box, attempting invis-ibility. He remained motionless, instinctively knowing that, if detected, he might be killed.

His buff-colored fur helped shield him. A person ran past with a dog. Neither noticed the cowering creature.

A man and his six-year-old son, enjoying an early-morning nature walk, sauntered into view. The young bunny stayed frozen in place, but the tall man spotted him.

Amos recognized that the rabbit was not a native wild one, and he knew that a domestic bunny would not survive on his own. After explaining to Chandler how they might capture the small waif, he and the boy began ambling toward the garbage area.

The terrified bunny darted behind the dumpster. Young Chandler spied him and started forward again; Amos circled around to approach from behind.

The rabbit bolted from one side to the other.

Father and son worked together, herding the rabbit, trying to get close. But the bunny was scared and kept scrambling away.

Thirty minutes passed. Then forty. The rabbit was tiring. Talking in quiet tones, Amos slowly walked up to face the bunny, leaned over, and gently petted between the rabbit's dark brown eyes. The little rex was too tired to run away and momentarily relaxed—just long enough for Amos to grasp him firmly.

Amos lifted the wisp of a rabbit and checked him over. The short fur was soiled and dull. The rabbit was too skinny; he was starving and dehydrated.

"He needs medical care."

"Let's take him to Grandma," Chandler said.

"He might belong to somebody," Amos hedged.

"He's all alone," his son countered.

"Maybe he's lost."

"Huh-uh. I don't see anyone looking for him."

The child's logic was irrefutable. There wasn't a soul in sight. Nor any houses nearby. Amos knew the vulnerable prey animal hadn't traveled to the area on his own.

They hurried to the car, where Amos settled the little rabbit on his son's lap. He drove through the nearest residential area, but found no one outside frantically searching for a cherished bunny companion.

Amos called his mother, Caroline Gilbert, founder and manager of The Fund for Animals Rabbit Sanctuary in Simpsonville, South Carolina. Soon they were on their way, taking the rex rabbit to his new home.

Chandler stroked the amiable bunny's head and back. It was obvious the rabbit enjoyed the tender ministrations—he snuggled closer to his human buddy.

"He's the color of toast, Dad. I'm going to call him Toast."

As though in answer, the bunny butted his head against Chandler's hand, wanting more caresses.

"Look, Dad—he *loves* to be petted." Then the

Caroline Gilbert

child's voice turned serious. "Toast would've died if we hadn't found him, right?"

"Yes, he would."

Chandler pensively stroked the soft fur, then declared, "It's good we took that walk this morning."

Upon arrival at the sanctuary, Toast's health checkup revealed digestive problems serious enough to make him a permanent resident of the health care building. Chandler helped settle the nine-month-old bunny, chattering to his grandmother about the rescue and how much Toast liked being petted.

The very next day Caroline verified Chandler's assertions; she found out that Toast basked in attention! The new resident was sweet and charming, and he thoroughly enjoyed having people run their fingers through his cotton-velvet fur. It didn't take long for him to earn the distinction of the bunny most often virtually adopted (meaning he never had to leave home). Chandler would visit and quip that Toast was one of his grandmother's best treasures.

But despite Toast's fondness for people, it was Emily who became the love of his life. A diminutive silver-grey rabbit, she was brought to the sanctuary by a gentleman who loved her well but who worked long hours and knew she was lonely. Because of physical problems, she was assigned to the health building. Toast instinctively sensed Emily's frailty and for several years was her steadfast companion, her comfort and protector.

When Emily died, Caroline was so concerned that Toast would become depressed by the loss of his beloved that she and other volunteers spent extra time with him. So effectively did Toast's human friends help him through his loneliness that when Roanoke, a head-tilt bunny, and Toby, an older rabbit with health problems, took up residence, Toast willingly extended his nose in friendship. The three friends began to spend their time together, inside and out.

Toast is an elderly rabbit now. Although he's somewhat creaky and less spry, age hasn't diminished his fondness for attention. He's one of the first rabbits that sanctuary visitors see, and he makes sure he gets what he considers a fair share of the petting. When Chandler and Amos visit, Toast gingerly hops over to be picked up. They're always willing to comply. After all, they were the first to recognize Toast for the treasure he is.

ABOUT RABBITS: vision

Although rabbits' eyes are structured to see well in dim light and to give a panoramic view, they are unable to recognize detail or to perceive a full color spectrum. Rabbits stand on their hind legs to identify surroundings, recognize distant objects, and discern danger.

Because the eyes are located on the sides of their heads, rabbits do not have binocular vision. To compensate, they "bob" (move their heads up and down) or "scan" (turn their heads from side to side). These movements somewhat alter their observational position and provide a new line of sight (parallax).

In addition, their eye placement creates two blind spots—a short one in front of their faces and a longer one behind their tails. The blind spot in front of a bunny's nose can lead to inadvertently biting a finger, especially if a bunny smells food or reacts to the "foreign" object as a possible threat.

Due to selective breeding, some domestic rabbits have eyesight that is further limited (in range and acuity) by lop ears, ridged brows, and bangs.

The Rabbit MaMaa Triumphant

Information for this story was provided by Ray Silja,
Stephen Guida, and Stacey Shirer

Some young kids found them: the mother rabbit and her eight newborn babies, boxed up and tossed into a dumpster.

The doe was skinny and dirty. Her kits, curled in minuscule balls, were furless, with eyes that looked pasted shut. The kids feared that some of the babies were already dead and, seeking help, hurried the box home.

The bunny family—each member dangerously close to death—was transferred to Brambley Hedge Rabbit Rescue. Founder, Erika, and fellow volunteer, Stacey, worked feverishly to save their lives. It was a relief when MaMaa—as they named her—finally responded with enough strength to tend her tiny babies.

But that respite was short-lived. Less than two weeks after being rescued, every one of the kits became critically ill. Again death threatened.

The vet discovered a massive infestation of parasites. Obviously MaMaa had endured horrible living conditions in her early life and had passed the parasites to her offspring. Medication was necessary, and Erika worried about the sizable risk of long-term effects to the young ones.

An entire week passed before all the babies began to show signs of improvement. A sense of optimism again filled the shelter.

Then—only twenty-nine days after the rabbits had been discovered in the trash—the still-thin MaMaa birthed more babies. The timing made it clear that MaMaa had been newly pregnant when she and her eight nurslings were discarded. The only bright note, if it could be called that, was that the new litter was small, due to MaMaa's poor health.

So that she could care for her newborns, Erika and Stacey weaned the first litter of eight, diligently providing the extra care needed at that young age.

But despite their ministrations, illness again set in and death prevailed for four of the bunnies. Among those survivors strong enough to battle the ravages of their early lives, some exhibited signs of congenital problems, making them special-needs bunnies.

Finally, good fortune conquered adversity. MaMaa recovered, acquiring self-assurance as rapidly as weight. Golden fur—highlighted by white—became a luxurious covering for her eight-pound body. Her remaining youngsters, gorgeous miniatures of their upright-eared palomino-mix mother, grew to health and were adopted. Although independent, MaMaa loved attention and was so sweet and loving that Erika and Stacey were sure that she too would soon find herself in a forever home.

But four years passed. MaMaa was continually overlooked in favor of smaller bunnies or lop-eared breeds.

Then, at long last, a special day. Brambley Hedge received an email from a man who had lost his beloved French lop, Janis. With tears blurring her vision, Stacey read, "Although I have a special affection for lops, I prefer to adopt any breed so long as the rabbit is one nobody else wants and is, therefore, unlikely to be selected."

She immediately wrote back, describing MaMaa and two other rabbits, and arranged to meet Ray at PetSmart on a scheduled adoption day.

⁓

Ray remembers his first sight of MaMaa: "She was lying down, resting her head on the edge of her litter box. She looked so cute and relaxed. When I walked up, she hopped to the cage door, curious about me."

He completed the necessary adoption requirements, and MaMaa finally went home.

But instead of feeling safe in her new surroundings, MaMaa acted frightened of everything. The sound of Ray clearing his throat sent her running to hide under the bed. The sight of a grooming brush brought a wild look to her eyes, and she'd attack, as though fearing Ray intended to hit her with it. If he made a sudden movement, she lunged and drew blood.

With sadness he wrote, "I suspect she suffered abuse at the hands of a male. It's going to take a long time before those bad memories subside."

But Ray persevered, even spending months sleeping on the floor with MaMaa to help her get used to him. It took over a year before she fully relaxed into comfort and security. Once she did, she blossomed!

She'd rise early with Ray and, before the desert heated up, dart in and out of the house, making a game of racing to the best hiding spots in the rabbit-fenced yard. Her guardian watched as she performed gymnastics, dug holes, and then snoozed under the sunscreen drape.

When it became too hot, she'd come inside, lying next to Ray so he could pet her while he read. When it was time for him to leave for class—retired now and working on a second advanced degree—she'd settle under a chair and listen to classical music on the radio, expressing contentment by softly grinding her teeth, a rabbit's method of purring.

Ray Silja

And she learned words and phrases. Many of them. Ray, whose eclectic background includes co-authorship of a book on literacy tutoring as well as research into animal intelligence, used frequent repetition to nurture and expand her vocabulary. He provided periodic updates to Stacey, extolling the intelligence of The Rabbit MaMaa, who also recognized her names, "Baby" and "Sweetheart."

Given affection and freedom, MaMaa has become a carefree, well-adjusted rabbit. When she's happy and excited, she spins in circles at Ray's feet. When she observes that he plans to lie on the floor and watch television, she gets in position for petting. MaMaa has turned into a cuddler who can't spend enough time with the man who respects her and holds her dear.

The two now share their home with a couple of Netherland dwarfs. Though MaMaa adores the small bunnies, she eschews their flurry of activity, choosing instead to sit with her trusted human.

Her days are filled with ease and joy—the adversity endured as a young doe long forgotten. Hers is a success story, and she is The Rabbit MaMaa Triumphant.

ABOUT RABBITS: reproduction

Rabbits can begin reproducing at a surprisingly young age. Some rabbits may achieve sexual maturity as early as 2-1/2 months, even though 4 months is considered standard. Rabbits should never be bred at a young age, as this practice creates problems in both mother and offspring.

Female rabbits do not have specific fertility cycles—no timing is involved. The act of mating causes them to ovulate (induced ovulation) and pregnancy is nearly guaranteed. The gestation period for rabbits is basically a month (28–31 days).

A healthy doe can deliver 1–14 babies; the average number born to a mid-size rabbit is 6 or 7. The first litter is generally smaller. A rabbit can become pregnant shortly after giving birth, but that is incredibly stressful and unhealthy for the doe and her kits.

When "same sex" rabbits are purchased, there is often a rude surprise when baby bunnies are subsequently born. This often happens because it is difficult to properly sex young rabbits. The fact that testicles of young males are commonly carried inside their bodies leads inexperienced observers to assume that they are females. Even if the male is immediately removed upon discovery of the "same-sex" error, a second litter is generally born about 30 days later.

Of course, all these situations can be avoided if much-loved bunnies are accurately sexed and kept gender-separated from the age of 10 weeks until spayed or neutered, at the appropriate age and by a rabbit-knowledgeable vet.

Born to Be ME!

by Bernie S. Siegel, MD

It was early spring, just a week after Easter. Two baby rabbits, purchased to adorn Easter baskets, had lost their appeal. They were still cute and cuddly, but taking care of them had become just another chore.

The children's parents didn't want the responsibility of caring for the bunnies. So, under the cover of twilight the two tiny babies, who could easily fit into a coat pocket, were abandoned in the nearby woods.

In near darkness, the defenseless orphans crouched together, quivering with fear. The rustling sounds, menacing dark shadows, strange and disturbing smells—everything about the alien place heightened their panic and instincts to hide.

But the two little sisters had no burrow to hide in. No food or water. They had no family to turn to, no one to help them. The dark fur of one bunny helped hide her in the darkness. The other tiny rabbit was white and her fur, illuminated by the moon, was like a beacon for predators. She did not survive the night.

The small black bunny, nearly scared to death, was left to face the nightmare of the woods alone. She hunched under a bush, paralyzed with fear and grieving for her sister and only friend; she was depressed, hungry, thirsty, cold.

Dawn came at last. The baby rabbit caught the scent of food. Heedless of danger, she followed the smell. It emanated from a nearby wire contraption where, upon entering, she found a bowl of baby bunny pellets. Just as her mouth touched the dish the trap snapped closed behind her.

The rabbit whirled around. There was no way out.

~

"She looks like a little black smudge," my wife, Bobbie, observed.

And so, in that moment, our rabbit was named: *Smudge.*

Bobbie and I had happened to see the abrupt abandonment of the two bunnies the night before and had immediately tried to save them. But since they were afraid and retreated further into the darkness, we set a humane trap.

Early the next morning, we hurried to check it. The coal-black bunny was inside, hunched down, trying to hide.

"We're buddies," I said as I opened the cage.

Her elfin body, so downy soft, fit into the palm of my hand. I'd never held a rabbit in this way before and was immediately awestruck. She was so perfect. I felt my heart open in wonder and gratitude.

Gazing at the vulnerable little creature, I marveled at how she sat so trustingly in my hand. She looked at me with her beautiful brown eyes, and I knew she was a blessing, and more—her presence was an opportunity to learn.

I was sure our four cats would come to accept Smudge, but I wondered how those feline predators would initially react to the sudden appearance of a helpless prey animal. Keeping our newest family member safe became my first objective. I built a sturdy, predator-proof, three-room bunny bungalow and secured it on an outside porch, in front of our windows so we could see Smudge at all times.

She appeared content and seemed to enjoy the attention from the curious cats, who liked to sit next to her home. After everyone became good friends, they shared the yard whenever Bobbie or I was able to watch and keep them safe.

As Smudge grew, it became apparent she would eclipse the size of the cats and become a very large rabbit. In addition, she was so congenial and exhibited such a loving and intelligent nature that Bobbie and I wanted her to be inside with us. And so she became a house rabbit.

What a surprise that turned out to be—living so closely with Smudge really opened our eyes about rabbits! We had read books and searched the Internet about rabbit care, but it was through Smudge that we gained a new level of understanding and appreciation for them. It was a startling revelation to find out that our sweet and gentle prey animal was also very independent, mischievous, and bold. Sometimes Smudge tried my patience, leading me on a merry chase before bedtime instead of coming into the house. Bobbie would tease, saying our rabbit was a lot like me!

One summer day we were introduced to rabbit communication. We heard a grunt—not a soft little sound but a full-throated, hoarse, growly sound, one that had Smudge's full fifteen pounds behind it.

Bobbie started and whirled around; I dropped the morning paper.

Seeing she'd achieved the desired affect, Smudge looked at us and grunted again.

"She must be hungry," Bobbie said as she hurried to wash Smudge's favorite vegetables.

"Maybe she wants to be petted," I responded and got down on the floor to caress her soft fur.

And that is how Bobbie and I were inducted into Smudge's training program.

We learned that our rabbit wanted to be fed at the *same* time every day! When her meal was even a few minutes delayed, Smudge would grunt her annoyance, fling her empty bowl through the air, and watch it clatter noisily across the tiled kitchen floor.

She also liked being held and cuddled *upon request*. I remember the first time Smudge obtained affection on demand. Bobbie and I were in the den, and I guess Smudge thought we were ignoring her. She raced into the room, vaulted onto my lap, grabbed my book and threw it to the floor! When I began to gently stroke her ears and back, she flopped on her side in a big body smile and totally relaxed.

Smudge was always forthright in asking for attention and love—and she always expected to receive it. I'd urge my cancer patients, many of whom have a hard time asking for love, to emulate Smudge's assertiveness.

Smudge's instruction didn't stop when we learned what she liked; she imparted other important life lessons. One of her greatest teachings occurred when I unintentionally let her come to harm. It happened after I came home from the shelter with a little abandoned dog, whom Bobbie promptly dubbed Furphy. Knowing that Smudge was a vulnerable prey animal, we were careful to supervise their interactions. Furphy was a playful and sweet dog, and we made progress with the training.

One afternoon Bobbie and I had to do a few errands, and after we left the house I remembered I hadn't closed the pet door. But I thought Furphy and Smudge were good enough friends, so I wasn't really worried.

When we returned home, Smudge was in her house, injured. Furphy had attacked her, and I couldn't understand why because they had played together before. Had he, in his exuberant dog way, tried playing with her as if she were a stuffed toy?

Smudge's wounds were serious and required surgery. The guilt I felt about this was enormous. My life has been spent trying to cure disease and help people heal, but because of my error in judgment, our loving, innocent rabbit had been harmed. I was the one who had wanted a dog and brought Furphy home. I loved them both, but I felt I'd seriously failed in my duty and responsibility to Smudge.

After she was home from the animal hospital, as the doctor in the house I provided all her care myself. Each morning and evening, I gave her medication and fluids, swabbed and dressed her wounds, made sure she was clean and dry, and hand-fed a special dietary formula. Even though I tried to be gentle, I could see it was painful when I tended her injuries or when she attempted to shift positions.

But Smudge never complained. Instead, she was grateful for my care and attention and would lick my hand when I was done.

Each day, I prayed for Smudge and visualized her whole and healthy. My guilt made the process a difficult one. Because of me, Smudge hovered between life and death, and I found it hard to feel joyful.

One evening, after I finished dressing her wounds, I felt the caress of Smudge's smooth tongue. I recognized her unconditional love for me and was finally able to joyfully and spontaneously smile again. I painted a portrait of Smudge and her truth was evident: she was whole and perfect, despite her wounds, and she was helping me to become a more complete human being.

Smudge became my coach and teacher, a perfect example of love and unity with life. At the time, it struck me that the word "wound" kept coming up in various contexts, separate from my life's work of healing wounds. This time, I had to work on that part of me that needed attention. Smudge helped close my wound, the one caused by guilt, and reminded me that blessings come in many forms.

Within a few weeks, Smudge was running and hopping again, with me in attendance. At first, she was afraid of Furphy, but one afternoon when I had to leave and wanted to make sure she was safely indoors, she amazed me by running over to hide behind him. In that simple gesture Smudge demonstrated that she'd forgiven Furphy.

I was so happy she had recovered that I didn't mind being led on a merry chase around the yard. Instead of becoming impatient, I welcomed the opportunity to see her exhibiting such liveliness.

One night, the moon was full and Smudge wanted to stay outside and play. I disagreed because I couldn't see well enough in the moonlight and her dark coat was nearly invisible in the shadows. But when she ran away from me, I followed. She stopped long enough for me to catch up, then leapt and sprinted away. I trailed after her. Again Smudge waited, but when I bent to pick her up, her speedy dash left me empty-handed!

It turned into a game of "chase me in the moonlight." Smudge showed no fear of the night, not even of the large shadows cast by the forest or the haunting and unfamiliar sounds that echoed nearby. She knew she was safe with me.

As the nighttime magic wove around Smudge, I watched my beloved teacher and friend transform into an enchanting dancer: she hopped, spun, and capered with her silhouette. Her choreography signaled her sentiments: "I'm wild. I'm free. I was born to be *ME*!"

And that was another of Smudge's lessons: that I, too, was born to be me, with all my strengths and failings, my loves and fears.

As Smudge danced her finale, I called softly to her. She stopped, rose up on her hind legs, and looked at me. In silent communication we stood.

Then Smudge ran and hopped into my waiting arms. Grateful for her presence in my life, I gathered her close and bent my forehead to hers. The realization that we were both divine children filled me with peace.

Together we entered our home.

ABOUT RABBITS: rabbits as easter gifts

Baby bunnies are often purchased as cuddly novelties to decorate Easter baskets. But as the small animals begin to grow, they often lose their status as ideal pets. There are some common reasons for this.

- Bunnies are frequently purchased on impulse and without adequate knowledge of their temperament and needs.
- Family members often lose interest after the novelty wears off and when chores become tiresome.
- As rabbits reach adolescence (at about 3-1/2 months old), they become more independent and grow more strongly into instinctive behaviors such as chewing and digging. As they mature, they may become aggressive or grouchy, especially if not neutered or spayed. At this point, family members may begin to view their impulse purchase as a troublesome nuisance, which can lead to abuse, neglect, or abandonment.

Help put a stop to the thoughtless tradition of purchasing live rabbits at Easter. No matter how tempting, never give a bunny as a holiday gift. Encourage family members and friends to reconsider if they are thinking of acquiring a rabbit at Easter. Urge them instead to join you in exuberantly declaring, "Make mine a *chocolate* bunny!"

Note: The Columbus (Ohio) House Rabbit Society established the Make Mine Chocolate! ™ *campaign to help educate the public about the problems inherent in purchasing rabbits at Easter. See their website at http://www.makeminechocolate.org.*

THE VALIANT VOYAGER

*Information for this story was provided by Beverly Endsley,
Dr. Jerry LaBonde, Bea LeNoir, and Michael Stein*

This rabbit will never make it."

My heart lurched; my stomach turned.

"I doubt he'll survive surgery on the abscess. . ."

My chest felt like it was being compressed in a vise.

". . .and if he does, I suspect he won't live more than a week after the surgery."

Tears flooded my eyes, obscuring the image of the pitiful body.

In silence, Jerry, my friend and trusted veterinarian, finished examining the pathetic raga-muffin, barely recognizable as a rabbit.

But the poor bunny looks better than he did a few hours ago, I reminded myself.

Hours earlier, I'd received a late-night call from a woman frantic to locate help for a rabbit who had dragged himself into her backyard. After receiving directions to our shelter, the wonderful humanitarian had driven over an hour to deliver the bunny.

"He's in terrible condition," she said as she handed me the make-do carrier: a box punched with breathing holes. Pale and distraught, she watched as I opened it.

My throat constricted as I looked at the dirty, skinny, stinky lump of fur. Ears identified him as a rabbit, but his lower teeth grew out from his face like tusks. Four-inches long, covered with dirt and feces, they stuck straight out. The top incisors, the same length, grew out to the sides like a strange mustache. A pus-filled, baseball-sized lump masked his jaw, adding to the grotesque look of his head.

Severely starved and dehydrated, the rest of the rabbit's body was a grouping of sharp-edged bones, every angle visible. Feces matted his fur; urine burn blistered his legs; bloody sores riddled his feet. Toenails were either broken or twisted in unnatural directions. Mite-infested fur fell off in clumps, leaving bare skin where his beautiful coat should have been. A black, tarry mess discharged from his ears, evidence of ear mites.

"Is he still alive?" The rescuer's question echoed her distress.

"Just barely." I could hardly get the words out.

Lifting the rabbit from the box would have caused him intense pain, so I cut away a side of the carton. The rabbit cringed, afraid of my hands—or of my mere presence.

He needed emergency care and, despite his distrust, I had to work on his pitiful body: administering pain medication, clipping nails, hydrating subcutaneously, cutting back the teeth, syringing food, medicating the rabbit's legs and feet, applying bandages, and treating him for mites.

I took him home, hoping we'd both get some restorative sleep. But my thoughts badgered me so that I couldn't rest. *He might not live more than a few hours. He shouldn't have to die alone. His last moments should be filled with gentleness and love.* And the ubiquitous, but pointless, questions that plague rescuers in any cruelty situation: *How could anyone allow such a thing? Why would anyone let a defenseless being suffer like that?*

Although the rabbit gave evidence of wanting to live, each labored breath seemed it would be his last. I was afraid to close my eyes lest he die while I catnapped.

"You're so brave and beautiful," I told him over and over as I gently held him, wanting him to know kindness, even if only for a short time.

He lived through the night.

"Bea?" Jerry's voice jerked me back to the examining room of the veterinary hospital. He was waiting for my decision, his compassion tangible.

He's NOT going to die.

The words impacted me from out of nowhere. I drew on their strength.

"He's not going to die, Jerry," I said with conviction.

He nodded in sympathetic understanding and quietly went to work. After administering additional fluids, Jerry clipped the fur, cleaned the skin sores, and surgically lanced and drained the abscess as completely as possible.

"Give him a bicillin injection every other day and bring him back in a week. I'll do surgery then," he said when he finished the procedure.

I was thankful Jerry didn't add the obvious: "If he's still alive."

Once home, I laid the rabbit's withered body in the bassinet that once held my child, healthy and so filled with life. Now in her place lay a being so weak he could not lift his head.

He's not going to die. I welcomed the reassuring words.

After administering his medication, there was nothing more I could do but give him a name—Buddy—and breathe a prayer for his safety and healing.

"Buddy," I sang out with false confidence the next morning as I peeked around the corner.

His eyes were focused in my direction.

I gave him time to become accustomed to my presence, then gathered him close, grateful he'd lived through another night. He rested limply in my arms, too feeble to struggle in fear. There was a quietness about him too, as though he realized fate had brought him where he would be cared for.

Very gently, trying not to cause him unnecessary pain, I began the intensive home-care regimen: fluids under the skin twice a day, syringe-feeding every few hours, medications, and changing the bandages on his legs and feet.

Buddy accepted it all in stoic silence as he teetered at the edge of death. Even there, he remembered fear. But he remembered life too: he'd try to groom his front paws and eat his food, signs of his strong will to live.

"You're safe now and so brave," I'd tell him, extolling his obvious courage. Somehow he had escaped from a living hell.

Beverly Endsley

I recited nursery rhymes, just as I did when my daughter was a baby: "If wishes were horses. . . ." I'd see a barely perceptible twitch and would cling to the hope that he was responding.

A week later Jerry performed the surgery, which exposed a menacing reality: the abscess had eaten into a large portion of Buddy's jaw. The infected bone had to be removed, leaving a gaping wound. After that, Jerry extracted the four rotted and malformed front teeth.

Buddy lived through the surgery.

When I arrived to take him home, Jerry cautioned, "The abscess was one of the worst I've ever seen; it's likely to recur and destroy Buddy's entire jaw." His voice softened, "Bea, you know how slim the chances are for a rabbit to survive this kind of damage. Given Buddy's weak and compromised state, he probably won't live much longer."

But despite the poor prognosis, the bicillin injections were continued. Although the standard rabbit protocol is one dose every other day, for Buddy the dose was increased and the protocol changed to a daily injection. He was in such grave condition and the chance of his recovery was so bleak that any risk inherent in this treatment was worth taking.

I did what I could to comfort Buddy and give him strength. If he lived, I knew it would be a miracle, and not of my making.

I watched his valiant struggle to live compete with the threat of death.

I gauged time in small, but significant, ways. Three days after the surgery, Buddy tried to lift his head to receive food from the syringe. He wasn't very successful, but he tried.

"Good for you!"

Another four days passed: Buddy lifted his head and then tried to sit up! He tipped over before I could assist him, landing softly in the bassinet, but it was a start.

WOW!

One memorable day in August, just two weeks and two days after being rescued, Buddy greeted me with bright eyes. I saw nary the slightest flinch of fear when I went to pick him up.

My softly murmured, "You little darling," merged into my sigh of relief and joy.

Three weeks passed. Buddy steadfastly clung to life, but he was still in very critical condition. As much as I hated to give him up, it was time for him to go live with Beverly and Kerry. They provided hospice care, and I knew they'd make sure Buddy lived the remainder of his days in pampered peace.

"We don't know how much longer Buddy will live."

Bea's words reverberated through my head with aching force.

"We are trying a new protocol, but don't get your hopes up."

It felt as though my heart were being wrenched apart.

"He may have a good day but then succumb the next. His abscess was very extensive and is likely to return. If you can just keep him comfortable, Beverly, until—"

Tears clouded my vision. But I could still see Buddy in my mind's eye: the feeble, bony rabbit who needed a loving, safe place to die.

"Kerry and I will do all we can," was all I could choke out.

With a heavy heart I listened to my friend Bea's instructions: bicillin injections daily, subcutaneous hydration morning and evening, hand-feeding regularly during the day, cleaning and re-bandaging sore feet, grooming his ill-smelling body, and checking for signs of the abscess.

After Bea lovingly bade Buddy goodbye, I took him home and helped my husband, Kerry, set up a padded cage. As providers of hospice and foster care for the Colorado House Rabbit Society, we'd done this many times. But never for a rabbit in such dire condition.

Buddy's pink eyes followed our movements, vigilant for any threatening gestures. Pale-gray nose and ears heeded any changes in our intentions.

Slowly I approached his travel carrier. I was a stranger, and Buddy had good reason to be distrustful of humans. He cowered, as though expecting blows.

Such evidence of abuse was nearly my undoing. My tears threatened to spill over.

No one should die without having experienced the joys of life.

The words came out of nowhere. I felt them to my core. Buddy deserved every chance to know happiness.

Offering promises of safety, I gently retrieved the little urchin from the carrier and set him on a clean towel on the couch. He tried to make himself vanish from his new, unfamiliar surroundings and, when he could not, began a horrible quaking.

Kerry and I got down on bended knees, making ourselves appear smaller. With feather-light touches, we massaged Buddy's ailing body until it gave up some of its tension. Before bed, we pushed the injection needle though his damaged skin, then offered a silent prayer for his survival.

The next morning, I couldn't bring myself to open the door to his room. *Is he still alive?*

Kerry turned the knob. Not until he turned to me with a smile did I realize I was holding my breath.

That became the morning routine. Wondering if Buddy made it through the night. Waiting for Kerry's smile.

In the evenings, we took turns administering the bicillin injections, grateful when the emergency daily-dose was replaced by the standard every-other-day dose.

Our days took on a pattern of sorts. Bea had told us about the nursery rhymes she'd recited; we opted to fill our house with music and sometimes I'd make up little ditties around the words, "If wishes were horses."

Buddy seemed to respond, or so we desperately wanted to believe.

My passion for oil painting took a back seat to caring for him and our other rabbits, but when I had time, I'd paint figures of shadow and light—horses for Buddy. Kerry worked at home when he could, sitting with the rabbits while reviewing architectural drawings. Weekends turned into "bunny spa" days, held in our backyard. Buddy lay in the grass while we, his attendants, groomed him with soft cloths. Odorous puffs of fur floated out from our hands.

We celebrated each small step toward happiness.

He began to relax and enjoy our attention!

We rejoiced.

Buddy took his first unaided step!

We were his cheering squad.

Beautiful white fur began growing in, and markings, once light-gray, turned to near-black. Buddy began to look like the big, handsome Californian-breed rabbit he was meant to be.

We were proud parents, snapping photos and showing them to family and friends.

One bright summer day we were sitting under the quaking aspens, watching the chipmunks run back and forth to their home in the rocks. Buddy started grooming his cute black nose with his forepaws. He remained upright and balanced the entire time!

"Way to go!" Kerry exclaimed.

And yet another unforgettable day: Buddy hopped around the backyard and ran through the large cardboard play-tube. Then repeated the accomplishment.

"Yea, Buddy!" We applauded his high-spirited antics.

One day in September, a few months after his heroic journey into the backyard of his rescuer, Buddy performed his first bunny binky. A leap into the air, with a twist. It was a fitting gift for my husband, who celebrated his birthday that same day.

But the specter of death, in the form of the abscess, was never far away; it was step-in-step with Buddy's improvements. We knew each day could be his last. But, oh, how we hoped otherwise. Our sweet little hospice fellow was gaining weight and his jaw was better. But Jerry, the veterinarian, reminded us that Buddy was still in critical condition.

Bea, who received regular updates about Buddy, suggested a perfect bunny companion: Savannah, a gray lop who'd been discarded by her uncaring people. Bea assisted with pairing the two rabbits and, as soon as they were good friends, returned them to our house. Sweet-tempered Savannah immediately began her healing ministrations; she nurtured and groomed Buddy, seldom leaving his side.

In early November, we took the bunny couple to be examined by Jerry. He was amazed to see the difference in Buddy and teasingly asked: "You didn't switch rabbits on me, did you?" He answered his own question. "No, here's the scarred area where the abscess was."

Then Jerry gave us the most wonderful news: the abscess had cleared. Death was in abeyance.

Our relief was immense.

Beverly Endsley

But Jerry cautioned us that the abscess could, and probably would, return.

NO! My mind closed against that possibility.

On a late November weekend, Denver's NBC-affiliated television station featured Buddy and Savannah on the morning news. Buddy captivated the news team and crew, especially after they heard about his valiant struggle.

Following the TV appearance and during the time we were screening potential adopters, Bea paired Buddy and Savannah with another bunny couple: Monique, a deaf head-tilt bunny who had survived against horrible odds, and her partner, Colin. It was a success—now there were four bonded rabbits to comfort and care for one another.

And then a perfect New Year's Day: I received a telephone call from a man whose Californian rabbit had died and who wanted to adopt special-needs bunnies. I described Buddy and his friends. The caller, Mike, said, "I'd like to adopt the four." There was more good news: Mike is a paramedic and also a pilot whose job it is to fly almost daily to Denver—the bunnies would be in able hands and also continue to receive veterinary care from Jerry.

I remember hanging up the phone, thinking, "These rabbits have certainly earned their wings!"

After all the adoption requirements were fulfilled, arrangements were made with a hotel near Denver International Airport. We arrived at the appointed time on January 19 and were shown to the room of Captain Mike.

"Buddy seems to be doing fine now, but the abscess could return."

I was stunned as I listened to Beverly and Kerry chronicle Buddy's life.

"Savannah and Colin are quite healthy. Monique and Buddy will always require additional care.

My heart swelled as I looked at the four rabbits who'd be sharing my Wyoming home. They were so beautiful, albeit frightened by the unfamiliar surroundings, including me.

"They're all very loving, especially Buddy. He's so gentle and grateful, all heart and spirit. How he ever escaped his hellish prison, we'll never know."

I focused on Buddy, looking at me. It was hard to believe that, when he was sick and weighing only a few pounds, he had dragged himself to safety. What a story!

It was after midnight before I gathered all the pertinent information about the four rabbits. At 4:00 a.m., it was time for us to leave. Hotel personnel were helpful and gracious; they peeked at the rabbits in the carrier and added their good wishes for a safe trip.

On the way to the airport, I told my four furry passengers about the aircraft that would soar into the heavens and take us safely home. As scared as they all were, I thought I saw Buddy's upright ears rotate ever so slightly. I took it as a sign that he was listening.

My long-eared travelers were strapped into their assigned place: the jump seat of the cockpit. Monique had had a seizure just hours before, so as a precaution I set an oxygen mask on "full" and placed it inside the carrier. Five miles over the surface of the earth, I checked on them: three were on "full alert." The fourth, deaf little Monique, seemed content, unaffected by the flight or the oxygen mask.

Maggie, my beagle-mix companion of some years, welcomed us home and impatiently waited for me to open the carrier. Her job, as she sees it, is to protect all rabbits, and she immediately conveyed her benevolent intentions.

She watched as I set up a special padded area for frail Monique, who was unable to hop. Then Maggie turned her friendly attention to the other three rabbits. I was amazed that within the hour, Buddy, Savannah, and Colin were following old Maggie around and exploring—no lack of courage in this bunch! With Buddy in the lead and me in tow, they headed out the kitchen door and into the bunny-proofed backyard.

This was January in Wyoming, mind you, and *COLD*! After a half hour, I called it quits and started my training program. "Home," I said and pointed to the door.

They pointedly ignored me.

"Home," I repeated.

In unison, three bunnies presented their backsides to me.

I think it was sweet-dog Maggie who convinced them to take pity on me. A few minutes later they were kind enough to dash inside so I could get warm.

The questionable effectiveness of my training program niggled at me—I wondered who was going to train whom. But, as days passed, it got easier. Buddy thought Maggie-dog was tops, so he followed her around. Colin, who suffers a case of hero worship, fell in behind Buddy, and Savannah brought up the rear. I carried Monique.

Socializing the group was an even simpler task: I enlisted the hearts, hands, and laps of my friends. Each lap was (and still is) assigned a rabbit. Even my card-playing buddies became involved—massages and petting were dealt out *before* attention turned to the game.

However, when my friends were not visiting, I had my hands full. The rabbits all needed regular, individual attention.

After I developed a routine, the rabbits established theirs. Buddy loved exploring; he'd lead and his friends would follow. He'd investigate *everything* and staked his claim by chin rubbing—leaving an undetectable-to-humans scent on those things, including Maggie, that Buddy considered part of his territory.

Then, without any warning, the abscess returned and Buddy took a serious downturn. For months, the abscess seesawed in and out of his life. Each time, I flew him to Denver, where House Rabbit Society volunteers assisted me in getting him to and from Jerry's office. Buddy accepted the medical treatment with grace, and his indomitable will to live brought him through. I found it amazing that he'd gallop to me when I called his name, even though it meant getting a shot. He was so happy to have his ears scratched and receive attention that he viewed the push of the needle as just another opportunity to spend time on my lap.

He became my inspiration and hero. Everyone who met him felt the same way.

Then, the abscess attacked again, this time with a vengeance. Buddy's body didn't respond to the antibiotics. That evening he was my jump-seat passenger on the trip to Denver. His former hospice parents, Beverly and Kerry, were waiting for us at the airport; they took Buddy to see Jerry at the animal hospital the next morning.

Jerry called me with the devastating news: the abscess once more involved the jawbone, and this time a back tooth was infected as well. He'd already performed the surgery, but my courageous bunny friend was in very grave condition.

Death was again a haunting prospect.

My spirits ebbed. Buddy was such a special rabbit; he meant the world to me. I wasn't prepared to lose him.

He's going to LIVE! The proclamation swept around me like the Wyoming wind.

I took the words to heart and couldn't wait to get Buddy home to start the daily injections. But this time, they were ineffective. Buddy's condition worsened. The large mass of scar tissue, remnants of the original abscess, became

Michael Stein

infected. I flew him back to Denver, where Jerry prescribed additional antibiotics, inserted surgical drains, and showed me how to administer a medicated wound flush. I couldn't help noticing that the vet's generally optimistic demeanor was absent.

Once we were home again, it was apparent that Buddy's bunny friends were stressed and worried about him. Monique was especially anxious to groom and help care for Buddy. She didn't like the surgical drains protruding from his jaw and started jerking on them, trying to remove them. I had to isolate Buddy from his best friends.

The infection continued unabated. I handfed Buddy, gave him antibiotics, but nothing was working.

He's going to live. I wanted to believe but was having a hard time keeping my worries at bay.

We took another trip to Denver. Jerry surgically removed more of the disintegrated tissue, inserted new drains, and gave me instructions to flush the surgical drains every four hours. The only way I could do that was to take Buddy to work with me. He became my jump-seat passenger, accumulating more than 30,000 miles and becoming a frequent flyer!

The infection was finally contained, and Buddy slowly began to gain weight.

I quietly but joyfully plucked some tunes on my banjo, creating melodies that fit the rhythm and rhyme of "If wishes were horses."

After six weeks, the drains were removed. Even though the resulting holes had to be flushed, we were making progress.

I happily shared the news with furred and non-furred family and friends.

After eight weeks, Jerry advised that flushes be done every six hours, rather than every four. A couple of weeks later, that was changed to every eight hours.

I'll never forget the sound of Jerry's voice when he checked Buddy after that long three-month ordeal. He was optimistic again; I could hear his satisfaction over the phone.

Buddy is going to live! I was ecstatic.

So were his friends. They impatiently waited for me to set Buddy on the floor so they could welcome him back to the group. Their esteemed leader had returned.

For the first time in months, I really slept.

The specter of death vanished. The infection, bad as it was, seemed a blessing of sorts. It "ate" all the fibrous tissue in Buddy's jaw and the mass disappeared. Buddy is in better condition now than he has been in years: he weighs nine pounds, has returned to his avid explorations, and participates in everything!

"Hey, Buddy, let's go." As soon as I say the words, he's right there with me, friends trailing behind.

When I constructed a small waterfall in the yard of our new home, Buddy pranced in and out of the pit, then decided to direct my work and sunbathe from atop the short mud hill. "Muddy Buddy" was his nickname for a few days, but he was a happy rabbit and obligingly sat through the several groomings required to get his coat white again.

In addition to our more active pursuits, he and I enjoy sitting in the stillness of the night. With fewer distractions of civilization, we experience the quiet and settle into the rhythm of everything around us. At times like that I muse about the importance of protecting all living things. As we stargaze I tell him about Pegasus, the mythological winged horse who, for some, is a symbol of the soul journey, inspiration, and wisdom. Sometimes I tell Buddy stories about canoeing by starlight. Nighttime is the serene backdrop to our daily life.

Buddy seems to cherish our special times together. He embodies kindness and goodness—a fact I find amazing, considering all he's been through.

His cluster of rabbit comrades has grown to thirteen now and, although not the largest bunny in the group, Buddy remains the acknowledged leader. Each time I introduce a newcomer, Buddy courteously extends his nose in greeting, shows the new rabbit all the best places in the house and yard, and then lays out the rules for peaceful coexistence.

Maggie-dog continues to watch over the rabbits, and since Buddy thinks Maggie is wonderful, all the other rabbits love her too. "Outside!" brings the fourteen single-file to the door. Buddy follows Maggie, Colin follows Buddy, and the rest, including Monique and me, line up behind.

When it's time to come back in, the reminder "Home!" generally results in the group lining up single-file again. The sight never fails to make me laugh.

Whenever anyone asks me about rabbits, I talk about Buddy because his story is so incredible. What started as a sad commentary on human nature turned into a wonderful example of people working together to save one small rabbit and make this world a nicer place. Somehow, Buddy made his miraculous escape. Then a kind-hearted person took action, and that single phone call started a chain of events that saved Buddy's life.

When I tell the tale to his rabbit friends, Buddy sits on my lap, licking my hand when I get to the good parts, cuddling closer when I talk about the bad. My favorite part is telling how Pegasus, the winged horse, came to Buddy's aid:

> . . . And then the brave white rabbit hopped onto the back
> of his winged steed named Pegasus
> and began his search for purest treasures:
> love and joy.
> His valor served him well as he determinedly
> made the long voyage home.

The other rabbits appear to listen as I extol the bravery and resolve of their intrepid leader, the valiant voyager who never gave up his search for kindness and love, who never gave up his search for home.

ABOUT RABBITS: their social nature (and binkies)

Rabbits are exceptionally social creatures, expressing friendship and love in joyous and heartwarming ways. They groom, snuggle, play, comfort, teach, and cherish one another. Having a furred friend will help a sick bunny fight to survive and will often make the difference between life and death.

A rabbit's need and desire to be part of a couple or a group may result in the bunny's bonding with a human, dog, cat, and/or guinea pig (cavy). He may even form a friendship with a bird, although some large birds (e.g., parrots) can be aggressive toward rabbits. In all cases, the human guardian must be mindful of the rabbit's prey status, confirm temperamental compatibility, make careful introductions, and supervise the animals to ensure their safety. (Be aware that being in the presence of ferrets is very stressful to rabbits, and that ferrets are likely to kill a bunny.)

When a rabbit is already bonded with a human, it is not uncommon for the person to fear that introducing a second rabbit will diminish the affection the rabbit has for his human companion. This is an unnecessary concern since rabbits are, by instinct, group animals and are able to share affection with a number of friends. However, to remain on the rabbit's list of close friends, the human *must* take the initiative and spend quality time with the bunny *every* day, at a time when the rabbit is receptive.

A bunny "binky" is a mid-air acrobatic feat. It's an expression of delight, a movement that demonstrates a rabbit's love of freedom and life. Each rabbit "binkies" in a unique way. A sideways jump, coupled with an air-spin. Ballet-like movements. A twist, twirl, and turn in mid-air. People have described binkies in many ways, all trying to capture the essence of the activity. A frolic in space. A small explosion of ecstasy. A wiggle of delight in flight. An expression of pure love and joy in the moment.

Snuggles

Information for this story was provided by Lucile Moore

"Never, ever, will I allow myself to be talked into this again," Lydia mumbled.

"*Never!*" she vehemently repeated, in case she hadn't heard herself.

As rabbit building supervisor at the county fair, she was responsible for the safety and well-being of her furry charges. The rabbit-judging event had just finished, and she crackled with frustration. What could have been a quiet, calm, and safe experience, for humans and rabbits alike, had been anything but.

It should have been easy enough. She had provided her requests to the county fair officials in a timely manner. Simple and straightforward, they were based solely on the rabbits' needs for quiet, safety, and psychological security. She'd asked that the judging event convene the morning before the opening of the fair; that it be held in a protected, contained area, away from crowds, loud noises, and rides; and, since show rules require the rabbits to be carried by individuals unknown to them, that the distance to the judging table be very short.

However, the officials' compliance with each of those requests had been either refused or rescinded. They'd scheduled the rabbit competition on the busiest day of the fair and in an unenclosed area.

Lydia had argued and cajoled, to no avail.

Arriving at the grounds early that morning, she'd been almost relieved that the dreaded judging day had finally come.

By the time the rabbit competition started, the fair was in full swing—a dizzy kaleidoscope of color, noise, movement, and odor. Hordes of people milled about. Voices of excited young children competed with booth vendors hawking their wares, midway music, and performances on three separate stages. The homogenized smell of cotton candy and fried food wafted through the rabbit building.

The first hour of the judging event went without a hitch.

But then the noisy crowd of onlookers just outside the entrance to the rabbit building really grew—not to look at the gentle rabbits but to watch hopefuls, young and old, test their strength with a sledgehammer. Most of the folks weren't even aware that a rabbit competition was taking place near them or that individuals were carrying sensitive, frightened bunnies through the jostling throng to the judging table. Lydia had positioned herself outside the door, hoping to thwart potential problems.

A young teen, holding a black rex rabbit securely in his arms, had walked out of the building and tried to shoulder his way to the judging area.

In one split-second, everything went amok.

A lucky contestant hit the platform with the sledgehammer, shooting the weight clear to the top. *CLANG!* The spectators erupted with cheers and whistles. The small rabbit, frightened beyond control, began kicking and struggling, intent on getting away from the threatening sights and sounds. Just then someone bumped against the youth, knocking him to his knees.

Lydia rushed to protect the boy and the rabbit. Luckily neither was hurt, and the bunny hadn't gotten away, which would certainly have resulted in his death. However, the gorgeous, well-proportioned black rabbit was now too agitated to be shown and handled.

After that, volunteers made a safe corridor of sorts and the rest of the judging went without mishap. But Lydia remained angry about the incident. The young man and the rabbit had been put at unnecessary risk.

The day wore on. She lifted her auburn hair from the nape of her neck, but couldn't feel even a hint of cool—just hot, dry, dusty air. The rabbits were such a popular draw that it was impossible for Lydia to move through the crowded aisles to replenish their water or ensure their safety. She hoped none of the rabbits would suffer heat exhaustion.

She groaned silently when the fair manager appeared, reminding building supervisors not to enforce rules that might antagonize visitors. "It's important that we reach our attendance goals, and we have to look ahead to next year. I'm sure you understand," he said in a condescending tone, looking down from his lofty height.

She was grateful when the supper hour arrived and the crowd thinned, albeit slightly. Entrusted with the care of nearly three hundred rabbits, Lydia worriedly checked her charges. The rabbits were showing signs of stress at being in such an unfamiliar, parched, and noisy place. Some of them, petrified, pressed against the back of their small wire cages, as far away from the mass of fairgoers as they could get.

The five-month-old black rex, who earlier had narrowly escaped injury, pulled Lydia's thoughts in a positive direction. He poked his nose under the For Sale sign hanging on his cage, begging to be petted. "Someone is going to be very lucky to take you home," she told him as she ran fingers of one hand through his plush, velvety fur and rubbed around the base of his upright ears. He signaled contentment by moving his teeth rapidly back and forth: a quiet purr, rabbit style.

"I'll bet you'd let me pet you for hours," she laughingly told him, "but I've got work to do. I promise I'll come back later."

She closed his cage and wended her way slowly through the still-crowded building, performing sight checks as she went. On her way back to the entrance, a red balloon hovering above the cages caught her eye. She knew it was most likely carried by a child whose parents had walked past the sign that specifically prohibited the objects.

Remembering what the fair manager had said about relaxing the rules, Lydia advanced toward the area, trying to think of a way to politely convince the parents to leave the balloon with someone outside. Failing that, she hoped this would be her lucky evening and—

BANG!

Her luck burst with the balloon.

The sharp pop was accompanied by the wails and sobs of a child.

The black rex rabbit, close by, began to flail in panic. Blind with terror, he slammed into the wire cage walls again and again.

His terror went unnoticed by the child's parents.

"Don't cry, sweetheart; we'll get you another," the father reassured his little girl, leading the way outside.

The incident had happened so fast. Lydia pushed her way to the stricken rabbit's cage, but even her familiar presence seemed threatening. His dark eyes were dilated; he was shaking so hard that she was afraid he might die of fright. But there was no quiet, safe place to put him.

An hour later, the young rex bunny was less agitated but still afraid. He crouched in the furthest corner of his cage, too scared to eat or drink. Ears pressed against his shoulders, nostrils quivering with rapid breaths, he shrank away as people repeatedly brushed by his cage.

Two young volunteers arrived to help feed and water all the rabbits. Lydia told them what had happened and

John Mead

warned them away from the black rex. But the boy, confident in his abilities, opened the door of the bunny's cage.

Certain that he needed to defend himself from the stranger, the two-pound rabbit lunged forward and buried his teeth in the young man's hand.

"Yeow!" The boy howled as he roughly shoved off his small attacker. "You stupid rabbit! I'm just trying to give you water!"

The little bunny huddled down, cowering in fear.

Lydia, knowing she must remain calm for the sake of the rabbits, spoke through the frayed edges of her patience. "He bit you because he's afraid. I'll take care of him."

By the time the fair closed at 10:00 p.m., she was exhausted. The day had been fraught with problems, the judging incident only the beginning. She'd had to contend with children who insisted rabbits love cotton candy or who wanted to share their hotdogs, or who poked the rabbits with sticks, trying to get them to "do something." Then there were the parents who thought nothing of letting innocent children stick their fingers inside cages or, worse, who opened the doors so their youngsters could pet the bunnies.

Grateful for the quiet presence of the rabbits, she set to work examining some of the ancient cages, formerly for poultry and still in use after forty years. She found bent or missing wires, loose floors, and weak doors. Afraid that rabbits would poke through a cage wall and start fighting, or fall out and break a leg or back—occurrences in years past, resulting in euthanasia—she methodically made every necessary repair.

The old poultry cages were stacked in rows, one on top of the other, so Lydia had slid a thin barrier between the rows to prevent urine and feces from dropping on the inhabitants beneath. It was nearly midnight, and she still had to clean the makeshift catch-trays.

"Deplorable," she said to her long-eared listeners. "Now I know why there's such a high turnover of rabbit building supervisors. You guys are wonderful, but the conditions here are awful!"

Before leaving for home, she made a final check to make sure all had food and water. It was much cooler now, and most of them were eating. Even the little rex, emotionally exhausted from the frightening day, was noticeably calmer. She gave his nose a quick farewell caress, locked the door of the building, and went home.

The next day was easier. The fair was nearly over and there were fewer attendees. Lydia had more time to visit and answer questions about the bunnies.

By late afternoon the midway was empty and the crowd had disappeared. Many of the rabbits were gone, claimed by happy individuals who had purchased them as pets.

When the fair was officially over at 5:00 p.m., people began arriving to take their entries—ranging from cookies to cattle—back home. Two hours later, the last of the stragglers headed through the gates. Everything was closing down.

The handsome young rex was still in his cage, the For Sale sign hanging lopsidedly from the wire.

Word had gotten around that he was a biter, a rabbit too aggressive to be shown in the competition event. No one had offered to purchase him. The person responsible for the small rabbit never came back to claim him. The fairgrounds were deserted except for county personnel. He'd been abandoned.

"Hey, Lydia, time to lock up and go home." A maintenance man, checking to make sure all the buildings were vacated, peered through the door at her. "They're getting ready to lock the gates."

"This rabbit was left behind," she told him.

"You're kidding!" he said in disbelief, then shook his head in disgust when he realized she was not. He mumbled something about irresponsibility as he moved off to check other buildings.

Lydia opened the door of the black bunny's cage and began caressing him. The rabbit pressed his chin to the floor and lay still. As he relaxed, she moved her fingers over his body, then took hold of him with her other hand and gently brought him out of the cage.

With one hand supporting his rump, she held him against her chest and gently stroked the length of his ears. The bunny nestled his head against her neck.

"You're not a biter at all," she stated.

His smooth, warm tongue lightly brushed against her skin.

"Well, you need a name. For now I'll just call you Snuggles."

In response, the young black rex snuggled tighter against her.

"Come on, Lydia. They're holding the gate for us," the maintenance man came back to remind her.

"Let's go home, Snuggles," she said. "You'll have good company! When the time is right, I'll introduce you to my

John Mead

friendly cats and to my bunnies, Timothy and Angel. I'll bet the three of you will be best friends."

Snuggles nuzzled against her and then cuddled close, warm against her neck. He was safe. He was home.

ABOUT RABBITS: county fairs

To reduce the stress on rabbits shown and judged at a county fair, certain guidelines should be established. For example, judging should be held either before the fair opens or in a quiet, secure area away from throngs of people, rides, and other entertainment. Dogs, balloons, and food should not be allowed in a rabbit building. A barrier should be in place to keep the public away from rabbit cages but allow access by fair personnel and care providers. Cages should be made specifically for rabbits, with enough room for the animals to stretch out and stand up, and with attached food and water bowls so they are not continually tipped when rabbits become frightened and move around.

Sadly, the conditions described in this story are not uncommon. If fair attendees notice problems as they pass by any of the animals, it is hoped that they will take an active interest and contact the county fair officials regarding necessary changes. If officials are unresponsive and if the situation warrants, sympathetic observers can contact organizations whose purpose it is to investigate animal-welfare cases.

As of this writing, Lydia Matheson reports that officials of this particular county fair have agreed to some improvements for the upcoming fair, such as purchasing a few new rabbit cages, but many more improvements are needed and higher standards must be established.

Bunny's Christmas Kingdom: Joy Uncaged

Information for this story was provided by Kimberly K. Dezelon

"Dashing through the snow
in a one-horse open sleigh;
O'er the fields we go,
laughing all the way. . ."

The merry sounds of the holiday classic matched my festive mood, interweaving with the scent of cinnamon as my husband, Michael, warmed nut rolls in the kitchen.

Our living room, rearranged to accommodate the decorated tree, provided the perfect setting for a lazy Christmas afternoon. I lay on the carpet, imagining what it would be like to see snow blanketing the city. But living in Phoenix, the only thing that would make our Christmas white was our precious mini lop, Bunny.

He must have known I was thinking about him, for all at once his full six pounds landed gently on my back. He crept to my shoulder, nuzzling through my long hair until his soft nose found my cheek.

HI! His eyes—the rich brown of maple syrup—sparkled in greeting when I turned to look at him.

His happy gaze reminded me of the first day I met him.

Our nine-year-old son, Brock, carried a plain cardboard box. "Surprise!" he and my husband said in unison as they opened the carton.

Out popped my birthday gift: an adorable, lop-eared white rabbit.

Already acquainted with Michael and Brock, Bunny was more comfortable than most rabbits would be in an unfamiliar situation. His bright eyes assessed his new surroundings, including me. Then he bounded over to say hello and nudged against my hand, asking to be petted. My heart was captured instantly.

Bunny sprang off my shoulder, jarring me out of my reverie. He navigated the room in short sprints, making sudden stops to examine items that caught his attention. He was our little explorer who loved to investigate; he was curious about *everything*! Only a week ago Bunny had "helped" me make gifts for the local rabbit rescue organization.

He promptly absconded with one of the small paper bags filled with grass hay and pierced with holes. After entertaining himself with the twine closure, he pushed his paper toy all around the room as he tried to access the hay inside. Finally, he impatiently chewed a larger hole—and sat, contentedly munching.

While he was occupied, I wrapped lightweight boxes, some containing a healthy goody. As anticipated, Bunny gave up eating hay and instead begged a treat. He then made off with the wrapping paper roll, butting it down the hall and abandoning it under the bed.

My thoughts were interrupted as Michael and Brock entered the room. After setting a plate of nut rolls and sliced cranberry bread on the coffee table, the two of them became engrossed in their new camera. Our dogs, Barkley and Sabrina, rousted themselves enough to sidle close to Michael, hoping he remembered to bring them a treat.

I munched a nut roll, idly watching Bunny. He was amusing himself with a twist of dazzling ribbon. I smiled, thinking about the night before: Christmas Eve.

It was just before midnight and all seemed still. I moved stealthily back and forth along the hallway, feeling very smug as I carted secret gifts to the tree. For once, my plan to exhaust our son had worked. He was sound asleep. So was my husband, Michael.

But not Bunny!

I saw a flash of white tail as he disappeared around the corner ahead of me. I entered the living room and burst out laughing. There he was, standing on his hind legs next to the Christmas tree, forepaws held sweetly in front of his chest. His sparkling brown eyes held an unmistakable message: You can't sneak anything past me!

I knelt down to arrange the gifts under the tree, but Bunny had other ideas. He bumped a bright red box out of my hand, herding it around until colorful curls of ribbon on a green parcel caught his eye. After investigating that, he nudged under a large soft package and peeked out at me, signaling his desire to play.

I stacked some gifts and made tunnels with others. Our excited Bunny performed binkies around the tree, jumped over his snoozing canine friends (who kept a sleepy eye on the merrymaking), dashed through the tunnels, then vaulted to the top of the tallest box, as if surveying his Christmas kingdom. The tree's tiny colored lights reflected in his eyes as he hopped from one gift to another.

When he tired, he crawled into my lap and snuggled close. Before his eyelids drooped, he nuzzled my hand to say, "Thanks"—just as he had done the first day I met him.

I enjoyed a leisurely stretch on the carpet and then sat up, not wanting to drift into a doze. I'd been awake past midnight and had hoped my small "alarm clock," Bunny, would sleep a little later than usual. But of course he, Brock, and the dogs rose very early, eagerly anticipating the opening of Christmas gifts; the remnants of our joy-filled morning were still strewn around the tree.

Michael selected the music to accompany our gift opening. The enduring English carol, "We Wish You a Merry Christmas," was the cue for our fun to begin.

"Good tidings to you
wherever you are,
Good tidings for Christmas
and a Happy New Year. . ."

As the words sounded softly in the background, I relaxed, content to watch my family open their gifts. While Barkley and Sabrina pawed their new fleece toys, Bunny tore his wrapped boxes apart, anxious for the papaya treats concealed inside. Then he joined in opening all the other gifts. He didn't care about the contents; he just wanted to play in the wrapping paper. As soon as there was an adequate pile, he began burrowing tunnels and bumping empty boxes into spots where they would provide the best cover. He cast aside the flat ones, trampled others in his exuberance, flipped paper wildly about, nosed over and under and through the lumpy, crinkly, multicolored mess.

Bunny enjoyed his splendid playground all morning. Finally, our darling little rabbit was so tired he simply fell asleep somewhere in the maze of his creation.

He was so entertaining, always totally immersing himself in family activities. Nothing I had read or heard about rabbits prepared me for the unexpected joy and hilarity that Bunny brought into our lives.

I got up off the floor, wanting a head start on packing for the trip to my parents' house in California. We planned to leave the next afternoon, as soon as the dogs' pet-sitter arrived. Bunny would go with us.

The little sweetheart was dozing on top of his bedraggled paper-bag toy. Much as I loved his antics, his "help" sometimes slowed completion of my tasks. I quietly headed to the bedroom, retrieved three suitcases and quickly packed Brock's.

I had almost finished my bag when Bunny appeared. Dashing through the doorway, he hopped onto a bedside stool and landed inside my travel bag, greeting it with unrestrained delight. He sniffed all the contents, proceeded to eject some, propelled others to one side, and then rearranged the rest. When my case was repacked to his liking, Bunny settled into it. He knew something wonderful was going to happen, and he wasn't going to miss a minute of it.

I couldn't suppress my laughter—his energy and enjoyment of everything were infectious. I gave up all thoughts of packing in an organized, timely manner and worked around Bunny's clowning.

We left the next day, looking forward to a wonderful family visit. Bunny sat in his large travel carrier, nibbling hay. When we arrived, he was somewhat hesitant to explore the new surroundings, but finally his curiosity got the best of him and he romped around the tree, repositioning and prodding packages into place. When he was satisfied with the new arrangement, Bunny took a seat among the parcels and serenely observed the holiday festivities.

My parents arranged the gift opening for the following morning so we could pretend it was again Christmas Day. It seemed I had slept only a short time when I was roused with a jolt. There was Bunny, peering intently into my eyes. When he saw I was awake, he hopped onto Michael's chest and nudged his chin. The eager rabbit waited until we were up, then jumped off the bed and disappeared through the open door.

Not wanting to disturb my parents, Michael and I quietly awakened Brock, and we tiptoed down the stairs.

"Dashing through the snow
in a one-horse open sleigh. . ."

The familiar music glided through the room. My parents were already up, watching our little white rabbit diligently investigating all the gifts. Bunny had amassed a group of packages and was singling others out; he looked like a busy little Christmas elf!

Brock and I lay down on the floor at Bunny's eye level. He took time away from his festal duties to hop over and gaze into our faces. His sparkling brown eyes held an unmistakable message.

What took you so long? IT'S CHRISTMAS!

Note from Brock Dezelon: "Dad and I surprised Mom when we brought Bunny home for her birthday. But Bunny surprised us all! He was so smart, quickly figuring out what we wanted and how to behave. We thought we'd have to train him, but we were the ones who really needed the training."

ABOUT RABBITS: holiday concerns

Holidays can be very difficult for household pets. The lack of normal routine, the visits from neighbors and relatives, the heightened excitement of children, and the frayed nerves of adults can seriously stress an animal to the point of illness.

During the holidays, it benefits a bunny (and other pets) to have quiet time, extra attention, and familiar routines as much as possible. It's also imperative to take protective measures for the safety and well-being of your animal companions. Cover or make inaccessible all electric cords. Do not let a bunny nibble on holiday plants, an artificial tree, or a cut or live tree treated with flame retardant, paint, or any other chemical. Prohibit access to water in the tree stand, and make holiday decorations (e.g., candles, tinsel, garland, breakable ornaments) inaccessible to prevent ingestion.

The Day Bunny Stole the Game

Information for this story was provided by Kimberly K. Dezelon

It was an ordinary Saturday. Ordinary, that is, for most folks. But at one house, where a white mini lop named Bunny reigned supreme, a new game was invented. Bunny made up the game and, of course, he made the rules.

I t happened while my son, Brock, was shooting hoops with his new basketball. The ball rolled out, close to where Bunny sat.

Something *new*! Our lop-eared rabbit sprang forward and stopped it with his nose. He pushed against it; the ball moved. He pushed again; the ball started rolling. Bunny butted his head against it, then he knocked it sideways with his body and nearly bowled himself over with the force.

Orange and white: the two of them raced across the yard. Bunny knew he was the center of attention—he could hear our cheers and laughter. He tried to straddle the large orange sphere, perhaps trying to emulate Brock. But the basketball just didn't cooperate—it was an embarrassing error for Bunny.

He kicked it with his back legs to show his displeasure, then dashed after the ball, rounding first and second base. A line drive, and they were at third. And while Brock stood watching, somewhat baffled by the rules to this new game of base-basketball, our excited rabbit stole home.

Brock tried giving Bunny a softball and a baseball, thinking a smaller size would be more to his liking. But Bunny was steadfast in his preference for Big Orange, as his game ball became known.

So on an ordinary Saturday, the rabbit who was already king of his family's hearts and home became master of the sports field as well.

ABOUT RABBITS: children and bunnies

Adorable, fun, curious, comical, loving—most parents would use those words to describe their children. People who live with rabbits use the same words to describe their tiny dependents, so one might assume that children and rabbits are a good match.

The idea conjures a very sweet picture. But the picture is often incomplete, neglecting some of the sober realities of the situation. Children's time with bunnies must be closely supervised. Rabbits are stressed when harassed, become ill when fed unsuitable treats, and are easily injured when handled improperly (including being picked up by their ears).

It's imperative that one or both parents take full responsibility for the family rabbit. Even if a child is unusually reliable for his or her age, still the parent is ultimately responsible for the rabbit's health and safety. Teaching children about bunnies begins with adults becoming informed about proper rabbit care, *consistently* modeling the appropriate attitude and respect for the bunny, and setting clear parameters to ensure the happiness, health, and safety of the rabbit.

Wily, Rascally Dave

Information for this story was provided by Caroline Gilbert

N ow what's Dave up to?" I wonder aloud as I make my customary rounds of the outdoor rabbit sanctuary.

I can see the part-dwarf scamp cutting up and reckon he's intent on riling his neighbors, especially the other male rabbits. Dave seems to know more variations of how-may-I-provoke-thee than I can count.

Sure enough, as I draw near, I see the angelic-looking rascal goading the newcomer in an adjoining rabbitat. Dave races along his side of the enclosure, luring his next-door neighbor into following parallel to him. Then Dave reverses mid-stride and, before the other rabbit realizes what's happening, the rascal is flirting through the fence with the newcomer's mate. By the time the confused bunny figures out the strategy, Dave is innocently engaged in grooming rituals with Juneau, one of the two females who share his territory.

Dave's apparent guilelessness is a sham—black ears and nose keep close tabs on his opponent's position, but he deliberately sits facing away from the rabbit.

Since I have time, I decide to watch Dave's machinations for a while. He is a marvel of a rabbit and always makes me smile.

The white fur covering most of his body is thick and luxuriant—it practically shimmers in the bright sunlight. He looks so different from the first time I saw him.

In response to a call, I had gone to a local veterinary clinic. Dave was lying on a table, his almost-naked body wrinkled due to dehydration, bone-thin from starvation, and mite-infested. Classic signs of extreme neglect. The mites had feasted on Dave's poor body: a large scab covered his nose so he could not smell, and they'd eaten into his mouth, genitals, and feet.

"What on earth. . ."

"He was kept in a small, stuffy glass aquarium in a school classroom," the vet told me.

"The children were allowed to feed him whatever they wished."

At the end of the school year, the teacher sent the critically-ill rabbit home with a student. Assuming by his appearance that the rabbit had a contagious disease, the child's mother wanted to get rid of him immediately. Another woman, looking for a companion for her rabbit, stopped by to meet the classroom bunny. She took one look, gathered up the frail body, and rushed him to the vet.

Instant countermeasures were started to try to save Dave's life: subcutaneous fluids, treatment for mites, special bunny food. After he was stabilized, the veterinarian called to ask if I had room for him at The Fund for Animals Rabbit Sanctuary.

Caroline Gilbert

I remember feeling horrified at what this six-month-old bunny had gone through and heartsick that the children had witnessed it. The neglect, the lack of compassion—I couldn't stop thinking about what the children had inadvertently learned.

I brought Dave home and kept a close eye on him during the many weeks he needed intensive care. He was too weak to be anything but a model patient, but once in a while I saw signs of returning health: a nose twitching nonstop, ears rotating to follow sounds, and a growing appetite. Even more encouraging, I saw glimpses of his strong spirit.

My thoughts are suddenly interrupted as fun-loving, mischievous Dave begins to sashay around, rabbit style. In an instant, he becomes an acrobat: he flies through the air, jumps to the top of his house and down, and speeds around his province, circling his consorts, Millie and Juneau.

The two large, white New Zealand females are a good match for Dave. Tired of his antics, they corner him and demand attention. The three groom and cuddle together, nestling cheek-to-cheek.

It would be convenient for me to do some cleanup in the enclosure now, but I hesitate—it's still early. Better to wait until the sun is overhead and Dave is sleepy. Otherwise I'll have to contend with his wily schemes: his attempts to escape, to seek out new adventures, and to obstruct clean-up tasks.

I decide to return later and walk to the gate to say goodbye to this personable rabbit who's a favorite of many. The alacrity with which he runs to me is dizzying!

"Boy, I could use some of your energy!" I laughingly tell him.

Dave stands on his hind feet and lifts his black nose for petting. I affectionately stroke his ears and the area between his eyes, then softly massage his jaw. He closes his eyes in ecstasy. I can feel the rapid movement of his teeth; he's "purring" as rabbits do when they are happy.

Assuring him I'll be back, I give Dave a final caress, then watch as he exuberantly dashes to the center of his territory and leaps to the top of his house, keeping a sharp lookout for opportunities to bait, taunt, annoy.

I shake my head. What a wily, rascally rabbit!

ABOUT RABBITS: in a school classroom

Rabbits are *not* a good match for the classroom because the nature, requirements, and realities of rabbits, and those of children, are diametrically opposed. If a teacher wants to instruct children about rabbits, there are ways to develop intriguing lesson plans *without* having a rabbit living in the school. Bringing a cherished house rabbit to school for a short time one day allows the teacher, parent, or other adult to model respect and love for the bunny.

At the back of this book is an article titled "Bunnies + Classrooms = *Mismatch!*" that outlines the many ways in which the needs of rabbits and children diverge.

THE RABBIT ROUND-UP

Information for this story was provided by Caroline Gilbert

We sized each other up—

Four adult humans;
three adult rabbits.
Each of us tipped the scales at over one-hundred pounds;
each of them weighed less than ten pounds.
We were confident in our ability to rescue the rabbits;
the small creatures were not about to trust us.
We pondered our plan and strategy;
they were poised and ready to scatter.

The rabbits had been dumped on a farm owned by my neighbor, Ann.

It was early on a cool, crisp October day;
gold and red leaves contrasted against the clear blue sky.

It was time for the round-up to begin.

We started with the black-and-white rabbit who had wandered toward the cows. Cautiously, slowly, the four of us moved closer around him, creating a barrier between the large cattle and the small rabbit. We took our time, trying to give the impression that corralling a dark-eyed bunny was far from our intent.

As we got closer, we hunched and stooped, attempting to make ourselves look smaller, less threatening. Even though our slow pace increased the chances of rescue, it felt like we were dawdling the morning away.

The circle closed. Squinting against the bright sunlight, my son, Charley, and I got down on our knees, then on all fours.

"Get him!" We issued the order to one another, simultaneously springing forward in what we now boast was one well-coordinated maneuver. After grappling a bit, we stood like Siamese twins joined at the rabbit, proudly announcing the obvious: "We got him!"

After settling the black-and-white bunny into a crate, we decided to capture the white rabbit. He had other ideas and began exploring a new frontier thick with honeysuckle and prickly blackberry. We tagged behind. The rabbit hopped a bit, then sat. Hopped, sat. We advanced. Darn, too fast—a blur of white flashed away. We tarried; he slowed.

"Pretty boy, good boy," I murmured reassuringly. But as we moved deeper into underbrush, it morphed into a plea.

"Come here, bunny. Please, come."

Good fortune finally joined us, leading the rabbit into a natural basket of loosely tangled vines. My fellow rescuers gently pressed down on the snarled mass, blocking the rabbit's escape. I scooped him up and held him close, softly stroking his head to lull his fears.

We were riding high on confidence, but the third rabbit kicked it right out from under us—the brown-and-white Dutch ran clean away. We hated giving up the rescue attempt; that little Dutch bunny didn't stand a chance of surviving on his own. But it was getting late and had started to rain, and finding him in dense thicket would be impossible. Maybe tomorrow, I hoped.

Back at The Fund for Animals Rabbit Sanctuary, I tended the two rabbits we'd captured. The black-and-white buck was in terrible condition. Long crooked teeth pinned his mouth shut: top teeth had grown into the bottom jaw, bottom teeth speared the top. The ability to eat had been out of the question. Knowing the agony had to be nearly intolerable, I performed emergency procedures: administering pain medication and fluids and clipping his incisors. After making sure his temperature was stable, I syringe-fed small amounts of special mash and wondered if his bony body would survive the necessary tooth extractions.

The white bunny was more fortunate; he was immobilized with fear and much too thin, but there were no signs of serious health problems.

Too early the next morning my neighbor, Ann, called again. Instead of telling me she'd found the brown-and-white Dutch, she starkly described a new rabbit: big, white.

No one else was available to help this time, so I hurried over alone. A terrified New Zealand rabbit led Ann and me on a roundabout. We soon admitted defeat, and Ann drove off to get help.

I perched on a boulder and watched the large, pink-eyed rabbit, who calmed now that I wasn't acting like a predator. In due time, he appeared comfortable with the arrangement and began contently eating his way along the creekside. This was my chance to make him understand.

O. Earl McCullough

"Mr. Big," I called softly.

The rabbit sat straight up, ears erect. In a magical moment I clearly understood him: My friends and I were crowded together in a wire cage, hungry and miserable. We knew there was no hope for us. Then suddenly, we were thrown out. We were scared, but realized this was our chance. We were starting to enjoy our freedom when you—

"You don't stand a chance out here," I interrupted. "The white of your body makes you an easy target during the day; you glow in the light of the moon at night. I promise that you can live your dreams, but you've got to let me catch you."

I knew that made no sense to him. How would letting me catch him allow him to be free? Pink eyes flashing, he sprinted away. Naturally, I followed.

Just then, Ann returned with a young neighbor, home on military leave. We three hustled along the boggy bank of the creek. The rabbit split left; we tried to head him off. He panicked, reversed, raced up the steep ditch, and followed the roadway up a long incline.

"He's bound to tire soon," the young man said.

I couldn't respond; I was too busy huffing and puffing. That rabbit would tucker out eventually, but I was already tired! And worried. The rabbit was becoming stressed by our rescue attempts. Then a new thought entered: what if a vehicle came barreling down that road? My fears must have reached the vulnerable creature; just that quick he veered from the road and leaped down the ditch wall.

We wanted to keep him in our sights. The young man began running after him, then yelled back to me.

"There's a culvert! He ran right in!"

A culvert? What luck! The cadet raced to the far end just in time to see the rabbit burst out at top speed.

"There he goes!"

But hope was instantly reborn. Another of the concrete drains was sighted; the white streak was heading straight for it.

Ann and the military cadet set off for the far end of the culvert, while I followed big white rabbit feet into the narrow opening. I was immediately greeted by claustrophobia; it hugged me fiercely.

I couldn't breathe. The culvert was just slightly larger than I was. It looked very, very long. I closed my eyes for a second. When I opened them, the space seemed even more intimidating.

My heart gladdened to see the rabbit in there with me. He was a big-eared silhouette against the circle of light coming through the far end. Maybe he'd let me catch him and back right out: it was a hopeful thought.

I stretched flat on my belly and began pulling myself along on my elbows. Progress seemed imperceptible. The rabbit hopped on ahead. Drat, he was going to make me go the full distance.

Inch by inch, I moved along. The skin on my elbows was raw and begging me to stop. I forced myself to visualize openness and sunlight as I continued to worm forward. Then the light went out; Ann and her young helper had closed off the escape.

The rabbit reached the end—no hops left. A while later I joined him—almost no breath left.

Whispering assurances that he would not be harmed, I elbowed myself still closer, trying to work up the nerve to reach out and clasp my hands around him. I hesitated. What if the terror-stricken rabbit considered my touch his doom? I shuddered to think he might emit that piercing, childlike scream, as rabbits often do in the throes of death.

"Please, please don't scream," I entreated.

Reaching forward, my hands firmly clutched his body.

He didn't scream. But he kicked and struggled until Ann and the young man reached in and lifted him from my grasp. After assisting me from the culvert, the two praised the rescue effort.

"Just like a scene from *Alice in Wonderland*," Ann said.

"A good military training exercise," the cadet enthused.

I didn't share their opinions. For me, it was a huge relief to be out of that suffocating space and to know the New Zealand rabbit was finally safe.

On the way home, I glanced at the huddled body on the seat beside me. The rabbit didn't feel rescued any more than I felt like a rescuer. He looked as though his dreams of freedom had been crushed. I felt like a monster. This would not do.

"You would not have made it on your own," I reasoned with him. "First of all, you're the wrong color; you cannot hide from your enemies. Second, you would have been doomed to starvation."

To keep my attention off my abraded, burning elbows, I told Culvert (it seemed the perfect name) about the good food he'd eat and play spaces he'd share with a female bunny friend (after he was neutered, of course, but I didn't mention that).

After a few weeks of getting used to his new surroundings at the sanctuary, Culvert settled in and established himself as king of his territory. His queen was a beautiful spotted female named Juniper Berry, who had been cruelly abandoned. The two companions played and dug, cuddled and slept.

Culvert didn't seem to miss his former buddies, but I made sure he knew they were safe and healthy, even the black-and-white rabbit. His front teeth had been removed, but he was doing just fine picking up food with his gums and chewing with his molars. All three of the male rabbits had kingdoms of their own. Never again would any of them see a wire cage.

Time passed peacefully and lazily for them. A year later, on a beautiful, clear autumn day—just like the day I first encountered the abandoned rabbits—I watched Culvert and Juniper Berry busily nibbling fallen leaves. They looked up when I called and happily ran to greet me.

Culvert's pink eyes glowed in the sunlight as he looked into mine. I'm sure I heard him say, My dreams have all come true.

ABOUT RABBITS: abandonment

Some people dump or release pet rabbits into natural areas in the mistaken belief that liberation will allow the rabbits to revert to wild behavior and live freely. The reality is quite different. Because of selective breeding, domestic rabbits *cannot* survive in the wild.

True wild rabbits rely on speed and wariness to survive. Selective breeding, however, has modified such traits in the domestic bunny, creating animals who are more sedate and more trusting of humans and other predators. Many rabbits live with cats and dogs and do not fear them. Selective breeding has also created particular body configurations and distinctive coats that put rabbits at a disadvantage in the natural world. For example, many rabbits have white in their coloring, making them visible, especially at night.

Even if rabbits are abandoned in an area with limited predators, they would not know the location of food and water sources and would die of starvation and dehydration. They will *not* form social bonds with wild rabbits nor will they be protected by their wild cousins.

The same holds true for bunnies released in an urban area. The fact remains that domestic rabbits have been bred to depend on human caregivers—they *cannot* survive on their own outside, no matter how lush the grass or how delectable the garden.

Turning a bunny loose to fend for himself is tantamount to the rabbit's death sentence. And a *group* of domestic rabbits fares no better.

Note: In this story, as well as in "The Valiant Voyager," rabbit-knowledgeable caregivers take emergency measures to save the rabbits' lives, including clipping the incisors. However, for a number of important reasons, treatment of dental problems generally should not be performed by non-professionals. Reference the article at the back of the book, "Rabbit Teeth: The Importance of Proper Care," by Dr. Angela Lennox.

The Great Rabbit Rescue

Information for this story was provided by Chandra Forsythe and Faith Maloney

Best Friends Animal Society has participated in large rescue operations, including the newsworthy 2006 rabbit rescue in Reno, Nevada. The following story recounts the original *Great Rabbit Rescue.*

The cold December day began innocently enough. Chandra Forsythe and Faith Maloney, two of the founders of Best Friends, were proceeding with their daily responsibilities of caring for sanctuary animals when the call came in—sending out ripples that directly affected their lives for months.

"I rescued a pair of rabbits," the female caller stated rather matter-of-factly. "They've had babies."

She explained that the two adult rabbits had actually produced two litters a short time apart. She didn't know how to determine the sex of the first babies so, when just a few months old, the young ones had birthed babies of their own.

"And now those babies have had babies too!" As she spoke, the woman's voice began to take on a frantic edge, escalating in pitch. "There must be a hundred rabbits now. I recently had hip surgery and just can't care for them all."

She described her situation, telling Chandra that even with the help of a hired man, caring for that many rabbits was nigh impossible. She didn't want to take them to a shelter for fear many of them would be killed.

She ended with the plea: "Will you please help?"

The tremor in the woman's voice gave clue to her anxiety. Chandra told the woman that she and Faith would drive to Las Vegas to check the condition of the rabbits.

Knowing the rapidity with which rabbits reproduce, Chandra scheduled the trip for the next day. Neither she nor Faith was prepared for what they saw when they arrived. Lops, rexes, harlequins, English spots, and many mixed breeds were all frantically climbing over each other for lack of space in the small enclosure. It was a profusion of color, fur texture, sizes, and shapes.

"Something doesn't add up, does it?" Chandra asked, referring to the variety of breeds that supposedly resulted from only two rabbits.

"Not quite," Faith agreed.

The creatures were in poor condition. Chandra observed open wounds, broken legs, chewed ears, missing fur. Old bread and rotting vegetables were scattered on the ground; some rabbits were nibbling on it for lack of anything else to eat.

"What a terrible mess!" Faith exclaimed.

"Worse," Chandra declared. "That horrible diet can be deadly to rabbits. Most of them are probably severely compromised and already have health problems. Gosh, how many bunnies do you think there are?"

"She said about a hundred," Faith murmured.

Just then the property owner appeared, using a walker to navigate the yard. A retired professional dancer, she explained that her surgery had made everything exceedingly difficult, even with the assistance of the hired man.

"Can you help with this?" she asked.

"First things first," Chandra said with determination. She extracted a promise that if the other founders agreed to the rescue, the woman would never again get more rabbits. The woman fervently agreed, offering to help pay medical expenses if Best Friends would take the rabbits.

Upon returning to the animal sanctuary, Chandra and Faith discussed the situation with the rest of the founders. The decision was unanimous: all the rabbits would be given a permanent home at Best Friends.

Chandra immediately began planning. Any delay would only result in more illness, more injuries, and more baby bunnies. She made arrangements with the woman's hired man and two days later, at the early hour of 4:00 a.m., she and Faith began what was to become one of the longest days of their lives.

Two employees, Carrie and Kristi, joined in loading four vans with every carrier they could lay hands on. Then the four rescuers journeyed south to the warmer climes of Las Vegas. When they arrived, the young hired man was waiting.

"I haven't fed the rabbits yet," he said in greeting.

"Good. Then they'll come up for food. When it looks as though a hole is vacated, stuff a ball of chicken wire into it to keep them from using that one again." Chandra reviewed with him the plan they'd worked out over the phone.

As soon as they began distributing food pellets, rabbits streamed out of burrows. They were in a frenzied, ravenous state, grabbing the food, scrambling over each other in the search for more.

Clay Myers

Faith and the young fellow began gathering bunnies. Each rabbit was handed to Chandra, who checked for injuries and signs of illness; then the bunny was passed to Carrie, who, sitting on an upturned bucket, attempted to determine gender. It was Kristi's job to place each rabbit in an appropriate carrier, keeping the ones who needed medical care separate from the rest and males separate from females.

Within an hour, everyone was hot, sweaty, tired, and beginning to feel both frantic and overwhelmed. They were trying to hurry, but they also knew how important it was to move calmly so they wouldn't increase the rabbits' stress.

Faith was the first to point out the obvious. "There are far more than one hundred rabbits here."

"I'm guessing it's nearly double that number." Chandra's face was glum. "The underground warren must be huge."

Fighting a sense of futility, the five humans struggled to move fast enough to get the job done and slow enough to do it well. They ignored their hunger pangs, gulped water, and kept working.

The entire frenetic experience felt surreal—it was nothing short of quiet pandemonium.

Glancing at the sky, checking her watch, Chandra calculated how much daylight remained. She became more and more distraught about the magnitude of their mission. She had wanted to collect all the bunnies in one trip, separated by gender, but there were more rabbits than anticipated. Time seemed against them.

"It's a four-hour drive back," Kristi gently reminded her.

"And when we get there, it'll be hours more before we have all the rabbits fed and settled in," Faith added.

"We're going to have to make a second trip," Chandra finally admitted. "We don't have time to sex them all either."

Given the short daylight hours and the amount of work that would need to be done once they returned to the sanctuary, the focus was on expediency. Chandra told Carrie to forgo determining gender and instead line one crate with towels, gather all the babies, and put them together so they could share each other's warmth.

"There is no way for us to know which moms go with which babies," Chandra stated. All the rescuers knew that rabbit mothers stay away from their kits except to feed and clean them. It's their way of protecting their babies from predators, since the mothers have a scent and the kits do not.

Carrie nestled together thirty babies, all of them pathetically thin, and then joined Kristi in placing rabbits in carriers. When all of them were full, Best Friends had one hundred fifty new rabbits to add to the fifty-two resident bunnies already living at the sanctuary.

"Faith and I will be back in two days," Chandra promised the hired man. "We'll take the rest of the rabbits then."

It was dark and bitter cold by the time the small caravan arrived at its destination. But their day was far from over.

Chandra chose for the workplace an old, empty building originally constructed for dogs. It was a cold, drafty place, with a single dim bulb that cast more shadows than light.

It was agreed that Faith and Kristi would find suitable temporary housing for the rabbits while Chandra and Carrie administered health care.

Chandra mixed formula for the thirty babies and, with Carrie's assistance, syringe-fed each one. It was a time-consuming process, as feeding babies too hurriedly could result in formula inhaled into their lungs, causing them to drown. But the pressure to hurry was unrelenting because the other rabbits needed medical attention, food, and water.

If only each of us could be a dozen, an exhausted Carrie thought.

It was with immense relief that the women finished feeding the babies and returned them to the crate. Struggling valiantly with the less-than-ideal conditions, Carrie used a flashlight to continue sexing the rabbits, including those checked earlier that day. Chandra began working on the rabbits needing critical care: the elderly, the injured, and the obviouly ill.

Meanwhile, Kristi and Faith covered what seemed like every inch of the three hundred acres in the canyon, stockpiling items they might need: fencing, surplus construction materials, heaters, nesting materials, non-chewable containers for food and water, anything they thought serviceable. They also located suitable temporary housing for the bunnies.

When they returned to the work building, they sectioned off space for those rabbits needing ongoing medical care and then set up heaters to keep all the bunnies warm.

Tired to the bone, the women felt there was no end to the number of rabbits. Focusing on the needs of each, pretending that every one was the only bunny needing attention, the women slowly made their way through the horde of furry creatures. It was a blow to discover that two rabbits had died in transport. Although both were old and ill, it hurt nonetheless.

It created additional strain to discover that the Angoras' coats were matted, some so badly they could barely move. Chandra weighed the benefit of greater comfort for the long-haired rabbits with the risk of shearing: the rescuers were tired and, coupled with the dim light, the rabbits' skin could be nicked or even badly cut. Unaccustomed as the bunnies were to the frigid nighttime temperatures, the loss of coat would have serious consequences. Chandra opted to cut through the mats to enable the Angoras to move more freely and to finish the de-matting process when conditions improved.

While Chandra and Carrie finished checking the last group of rabbits, Faith and Kristi began transporting bunnies to their new temporary spaces and providing food and water. Tall cat cages, large crates, and sectioned-off areas were utilized; rabbits were placed in the existing bunny building, a horse barn, maintenance sheds, and at Faith's house. Those needing special medical attention moved home with Chandra.

It was closer to dawn than midnight when the women finally hauled their cold, exhausted bodies to their own beds.

That was the beginning of many days of long, hard work. The babies needed regular feedings twice a day. Because of the caution required, it took hours to feed them. The other

Clay Myers

rabbits required grass hay, pellets, vegetables, and fresh water. Their living areas needed to be cleaned, nails had to be clipped, and ill and injured rabbits required medical care. It was a nearly overwhelming job that never seemed to diminish.

In fulfillment of the earlier promise, Chandra and Faith had returned to Las Vegas and picked up the remaining twenty-eight rabbits, bringing the total rescued to one hundred seventy-eight. Chandra's daily rounds of the new rabbit community were barely routine when she first discovered baby bunnies, born to females already pregnant at the time of rescue. Within four weeks of being brought to the sanctuary, the does produced an additional ninety-five rabbits.

"At least I know who the mothers are!" Chandra exclaimed in relief. She was happy to see them providing such good care to their kits.

 But her good spirits were dashed almost immediately. One morning she discovered that one rabbit out of the original one hundred seventy-eight had been wrongly sexed. Just *one*. That little boy bunny sired litters with all of the females he was living with.

Four weeks later, there were forty more babies!

In all, Best Friends ended up with a total of three hundred thirteen rescued rabbits. The founders tagged the effort The (Original) Great Rabbit Rescue.

After many weeks of hard, seemingly endless work, the day came when Chandra suddenly realized she was looking at more than three hundred healthy, happy rabbits gamboling with their friends and thriving. Watching individual rabbits heal from disease and injury had been rewarding. But seeing the whole group enjoying life suddenly filled her with the sense of a job well done, definitely worth the struggle involved. In spirit, she joined the rabbits in their joyous dance.

The serenity of working with the rabbits began to fill Chandra's days. She was no longer just caring for them; they were giving back to her as well.

"They touched my life in ways that are hard to explain," she once said. "Somehow, you can't be connected to a rabbit and still be stressed out."

Faith had echoed her sentiments: "Rabbits emanate such peace."

ABOUT RABBITS: overpopulation

A rabbit rescue often involves a sizable number of creatures because rabbits multiply very quickly. They begin reproduction at a young age, the act of mating *causes* the female to ovulate, their gestation period is short, and they can become pregnant again shortly after delivery.

When asked about the feasibility of Best Friends Animal Society bringing a large number of rabbits to the sanctuary in the future, Faith Maloney, co-founder and Animal Care Consultant, replied:

"It is doubtful that we will add more to our current population here at the sanctuary, but it's likely we'll assist in other rabbit rescue operations. For example, in 2006 we stepped in to help over 1,600 rabbits in Reno, Nevada. Their caretaker had become ill so we set up an off-site facility to care for and spay or neuter the rabbits before placing them in suitable homes or other sanctuaries.

"However, animal rescue is only a stopgap measure. We need a real *solution* to unwanted pets and pet overpopulation. Many animal lovers are working toward three main objectives, which also happen to be the thrust of our No More Homeless Pets campaign:

- encourage spay/neuter programs,
- promote animal ethics and humane education, and
- support adoption programs so that *all* healthy animals, regardless of age, can be placed in good homes.

"When a rescue situation arises, Best Friends works with other organizations in the particular region, and each group does what it can, depending on resources available. If the undertaking is very large, or if several rescues happen during the same time period and/or in the same region, most likely there would be too many bunnies for effective care.

"I can't emphasize enough the importance of spaying and neutering. If rabbits are not altered, there is no rabbit organization or sanctuary, or even a group of organizations, that has enough space or can provide adequate care for all the unwanted bunnies.

"But together, we can all work toward the day when there will truly be no more homeless pets."

Bunzo

Information for this story was provided by Debby Widolf

Bunzo was obviously ill. His tiny body was rigid, his eyes glassy. Each breath seemed a monumental effort. I reached into the cage at the emergency veterinary clinic and lightly stroked the sweet face of my four-ounce bunny. I was trying to comfort him—and myself.

The veterinarian returned from looking at Bunzo's chest x-rays.

"I'm sorry, but your little rabbit has pneumonia. His physical condition suggests he's been sick for several weeks."

The words shivered fear all the way to my toes; my stomach clutched. Bunzo was only five weeks old. I was afraid he wouldn't survive the illness.

"Please try, little one," I pleaded.

It was a Saturday night. I felt lucky to find an emergency veterinarian knowledgeable about treating rabbits. I tagged along with him as Bunzo was transferred into the animal intensive care unit. The veterinarian explained that the temperature would be controlled to keep Bunzo warm and oxygen would be pumped in to help him breathe. Antibiotics would be administered two ways: nebulized into the air of the chamber and injected into his body.

At least he'd have a fighting chance at survival. But the veterinarian cautioned that pneumonia is often fatal for a rabbit, especially one as young and frail as Bunzo. I knew the medications could also have a deleterious effect on his immature body.

"Keep fighting," I whispered.

I had to leave Bunzo at the emergency clinic that night. In the morning, he'd be transferred to an animal hospital for three days of care. I was leaving with empty arms; my heart felt as though it were breaking.

The next afternoon Bunzo showed very little improvement, and I felt discouraged. After spending time with him, I walked aimlessly, remembering my first sight of the little guy. It was hard to believe that it had been just the week before that I strolled toward a department store at the mall. I had taken one impulsive peek as I passed a pet shop. . . and there he was, cowering in a glass aquarium, trying to hide from the snake coiled in the cage next to his. As I walked up, the large, beautiful bird perched on the bunny's other side voiced a raucous greeting. The bunny quailed at the strident sound.

I focused on the dainty black rabbit with a white diamond on his nose. He was a soft ball of fluff and so cute, just about the sweetest thing I'd ever set eyes on! And so tiny!

My heart was his at first sight. I heard myself saying, "Will you put a hold on him for ten minutes while I go next door? Don't sell him to anyone else!"

After we arrived home and Bunzo was settled in, I began researching rabbit care. I was relieved to find answers to many questions the pet-store clerk had been unsure about. Three basics were at the top of my agenda: proper diet, litter training, and Bunzo's safety as he explored new surroundings.

Meanwhile, my impetuous purchase turned into a real bundle of joy! Bunzo bounced around the house, nosing his way into anything and everything he could reach (after I rabbit-proofed, that is). Each day, though, he seemed less lively.

And then he went deathly still.

Now, only a week after I brought him home, I found myself praying Bunzo would survive and brighten my life once again.

On day four, I was delighted when my bunny's status changed from hospital patient to at-home convalescent. But he didn't hop or move around; he just sat stock-still, accepting my nursing care and politely taking his medication in a very unrabbit-like manner.

In a panic, I sought answers. A phone call to the veterinarian brought a prediction of improvement in another week. Sure enough, six days later my adorable bunny took his first tentative steps.

But it was three months before Bunzo was fully recovered. My spontaneous pet store visit had become a frightening and expensive lesson: Bunzo turned out to be a seven-hundred-dollar purchase!

While I nursed Bunzo back to health, I continued to research bunny care and learned the sad truth about his early life. Like many pet-store bunnies, he was weaned from his mother too soon and then his needs were overlooked by the pet store staff. The glass aquarium in which he had been displayed provided inadequate ventilation and had robbed Bunzo's tiny lungs of clean air. I shook my head, remembering that he was housed next to a predator and a clamorous bird. I could imagine how those emotional stresses could also undermine his immune system. The cumulative result of his upbringing was a small body too weak to resist illness.

I vowed that Bunzo would have every opportunity to live a long, happy life, no matter the cost. I repeated my pledge often.

My little one regained strength and started growing; his curiosity, however, outpaced his size. I'd be fawning over him and all of a sudden he'd dart across the room to check out some new object. Or the dryer would chime, and he'd dash to the laundry room, jumping into the clothes basket to play. He loved the sound of the toaster, insisted on helping me make beds, explored every inch of the house, and delighted in finding secret places to take naps.

Bunzo was less than pleased, however, when I visited a rabbit rescue shelter and adopted the "perfect" bunny companion for him. Jasmine, a baby English spot, had been abandoned along with her nine brothers and sisters in Sandia National Forest, east of Albuquerque, New Mexico. Before a Forest Service worker happened upon them, six of the infants had been killed. Jasmine and three littermates were still alive, but wounded and scared.

In her new home, she turned her fears on Bunzo, biting his ear in introduction! My plan was for them to become friends and play together while I was at work. Instead, they hated one another.

But I was more determined than they were; I would *overcome* their enmity. For over two months, my days followed a pattern. Every morning the rabbits had supervised time together. It never failed: I had to separate them almost immediately. Each evening, I took them for a car ride, which created just enough anxiety for them to proclaim a short truce.

One day a rackety truck passed us, causing the two bunnies to seek comfort from each other. Then, Jasmine licked Bunzo's ear, the same one she'd bitten just months before.

"Omigosh, this is going to work!"

Debby Widolf

My loud exclamation startled the rabbits, who looked at me as though I was in the same league as the noisy truck.

When we returned home, I highlighted the date in red on the calendar. According to my calculation, it had taken sixty-five days for Bunzo and Jasmine to forge a friendship. They became inseparable and would lie cheek-to-cheek in beautiful contrast. He was coated in black, with a white nose. She was clothed in white, with some black spots, black ears, and a black nose. Bunzo would race to greet me, giving me a lick to tell me he was happy; Jasmine would race after him, giving him a lick to tell him she loved him. He was gentle and playful and never bit or scratched; she was gentle too, until I had to give Bunzo some medication—then she'd nip me, telling me to be careful with her best friend.

The two of them enlivened the house with their big personalities. They were inquisitive, sweet, sometimes mischievous rabbits who never missed an opportunity to play. Almost anything could be an invitation to leap into action. Their jubilant dance recitals were part ballet, part stunt, and part razzle-dazzle.

Every time I looked at Bunzo and Jasmine, I smiled. What an introduction they provided to the wonderful world of rabbits!

Over the years, many rabbits have enhanced my life, all adopted from shelters or rabbit rescue groups. All are a part of Bunzo's impressive legacy.

And for that I thank him, my black beauty boy.

ABOUT RABBITS: before bringing a bunny home

Small rabbits look like a bundle of love, with their innocent expressions, plush fur, and quiet mannerisms. To many people, the petite animals look like darling little toys. This response leads to bunnies being marketed as cute, cuddly, soft, and sweet.

Seldom are new rabbit parents aware of the real personalities and essential requirements of bunnies. They are high-maintenance pets, with needs that are very different from those of cats and dogs.

Before bringing home a newly adopted or purchased rabbit, research diet, health, behavior, socialization, housing, bunny-proofing, proximity to appropriate vet care—everything! Gather information by accessing reputable sites on the Internet and good books on domestic companion rabbits. Other good sources of information are rabbit rescue groups and rabbit-knowledgeable veterinarians.

If you decide to share your home with a rabbit companion, remember that many bunnies, including purebreds, end up in animal shelters after their cute baby stage ends and adolescent behaviors begin. If not adopted or transferred to a rescue group, many shelters euthanize them due to space constraints and other issues. Also consider rabbit rescue organizations or pet stores associated with a good rescue group.

LOBO AND BLUEBERRY

Dedicated to the memory of the Little Brown Rabbit

Information for this story was provided by Kay G. Fritzsche

M Y BUNNY!"
Five-year-old Alexa sobbed uncontrollably as she sat on the dusty ground. Her mother had taken the little brown rabbit and placed him where they had found him, huddled next to the petting zoo fence. Alexa did not want to leave the frightened, quivering little creature. She scooted across the dirt and put her arm protectively around the rabbit. "*My* bunny," she softly whimpered.

It was hot—one of the dog days of summer. A too-hot-for-bare-feet kind of day. No breeze, not a cloud in the sky, sweltering. The little rabbit squeezed next to the fence, trying to find a tiny bit of shade and stay out of the way of other animals.

Alexa's parents felt sorry for the bunny at the petting zoo. It seemed dangerous for the small, defenseless creature to be penned with ostriches, goats, and a menagerie of other creatures. But it was time for the family to leave, and they didn't see an official with whom to discuss the rabbit.

Trying to explain to Alexa why she couldn't keep the rabbit proved useless. The young child cried all the way home and for days afterward talked about nothing but the little brown rabbit.

Alexa's mother, Kay, began reading books and searching the Internet for information about rabbits. The family's two large cats posed her greatest worry. After discussing her concerns with rabbit-knowledgeable people and receiving assurances that rabbits and cats often become friends, Kay and her husband surprised their daughter with a bunny for her birthday.

When Alexa saw the slate-blue, lop-eared bunny, she was ecstatic! But the three-month-old animal was frightened and cowered in his cage. He'd been taken from his rabbit family and was now in a room full of strangers.

As she had done with the little brown rabbit at the petting zoo, Alexa gently stroked the bunny's ears and back. She soothed his fears and made sure the curious cats didn't get too close.

Within days the new family member was romping around the house. Alexa pranced after him and was quick to tell everyone, "He's *my* bunny."

Alexa named her little friend Blueberry and solemnly pledged to help take care of him. When Kay explained that rabbits can be injured if not held properly, Alexa agreed not to pick him up or carry him around the house. The very idea that her beautiful bunny could be hurt scared her. She promised to always sit on the floor before coaxing Blueberry to her lap.

But Alexa didn't forget about the little brown rabbit. She reminded her mother that he had been lonely and pleaded to return to the petting zoo to get him. If the brown bunny lived with them, she reasoned, Blueberry would have a playmate when she was at school.

Meanwhile, Blueberry demonstrated the same desire for a furry friend. With Alexa hovering protectively, he began circling Lobo, one of the family cats. The gentle giant watched with interest as Blueberry stopped in front of him, "presented" by lowering his head, and waited. Getting no response, Blueberry repeated his friendly rabbit routine, intent on establishing a bond with the big cat. But Lobo, puzzled by the lop-eared creature's behavior, simply watched, not understanding that Blueberry was asking to be groomed.

One day, Alexa hurried her mother into the foyer. There, sharing Lobo's favorite sun spot, the two animals slept side by side. Now, in addition to his doting human family, Blueberry had a furry buddy.

It was Blueberry who initiated the next level of friendship—he began grooming Lobo's large feet. When Blueberry lowered his head, Lobo responded with brotherly love and began licking behind Blueberry's ears. But the cat's raspy tongue tangled in the soft, downy fur, causing the floppy ears to bounce and flap wildly. Still, Lobo kept on licking, determined to be a good grooming partner.

Blueberry appreciated Lobo's efforts and reciprocated with gusto. He closely bonded with the big cat, followed him everywhere, and always slept with him.

The day old Lobo died, part of Blueberry died too. He was bereft without his best friend. No one—not even the family's new cat—could spark any interest in the despondent rabbit.

It seemed Blueberry would die of grief. With hope in their hearts, his family adopted a beautiful black rabbit from the House Rabbit Society. It was love at first sight! Blueberry didn't care that his new mate loathed cats. He didn't mind that she disliked the favorite place he'd shared with Lobo. He eagerly welcomed Emma to his home, glad to finally be someone's hus-bunn. Blueberry was in love and his life was complete.

Emma adored Blueberry, too. She demonstrated it, in part, by not allowing the family cats in the room she considered her and her mate's home. If one of the felines attempted to enter, Emma grunted and chased after the cat, intent on biting the intruder. As soon as the cat left the rabbits' room, Emma would race back to Blueberry's side and cuddle. The two became inseparable.

The family that had become "hooked on rabbits" celebrated! They toasted the love of Blueberry and Emma; they saluted the memories of Lobo and the little brown rabbit. When Alexa and her parents think back to the day they met him, their hearts ache. They keenly remember how frightened the beautiful brown bunny was whenever a larger animal came too close. They also remember how hot it was, but at the time they didn't realize that rabbits easily succumb to heat exhaustion.

But Alexa knows the little bunny is safe now. On a clear night she points to a special star. Whenever it appears to twinkle, she says it's the little brown rabbit doing a bunny binky. She knows he's never lonely or afraid anymore because there, in the star sparkling closest to him, is a constant companion: Lobo, the special cat who is a friend to all rabbits.

ABOUT RABBITS: petting zoos, county fairs, and carnivals

Petting zoos, county fairs, and carnivals all present similar stressors that may trigger a bunny's fears and affect a rabbit's health: unfamiliar noises and smells, mishandling by strangers, the presence of and potential injury by larger animals, and exposure to generally unclean facilities and all types of weather. Some rabbits, due to their nervous temperaments, should never be in attendance at these locations; they are particularly subject to illness due to the high stress and are exceptionally prone to injury when they panic.

Carnivals that offer rabbits as "prizes" generally offer adorable babies who are so young they cannot survive without special care. Unfortunately, most people do not have the specialized knowledge necessary to save the lives of such delicate, tiny beings. In addition, carnival-goers are awarded these living prizes whether or not they can provide a good home, know anything about caring for rabbits, or even want a bunny.

The Priceless Tulip

In memory of Courtney McCarty Johnson, who provided information for this story

He was dying of neglect. I knew it as soon as I saw him. One of the other volunteers at our animal shelter quietly confided that three other bunnies recently brought in had died when they didn't receive proper care at our facility.

Anger fragmented my peaceful state. I wanted to shout my frustration at the inadequate attention given the tiny, furry dependent.

Instead, I carefully lifted the two-month-old bunny out of the cage. He was puny, just fur stretched over a skeleton. Stitched wounds ran along his back; some brown hair was just beginning to grow around them.

I cleaned diarrhea from the rabbit's belly, hips, and legs, then situated the uncomplaining sweetheart in a towel-lined box and offered him enticing, hand-made whimsies. While he poked at the playthings, I scrubbed out and refilled his water and food containers.

Gently picking him up, I nestled the small body in the curve of my jaw and neck. What a cuddly package of sweetness he was! He squirmed into a more comfortable position; his ears tickled my chin as I lightly rubbed his jaw and stroked his face.

He wiggled with pleasure, which delighted me too.

I contemplated returning him to his cage, but worries filled me. It would be two days before I could return. *Who would make sure he was properly fed? Who would administer the prescribed doses of medication at the right times? Would he have play time or remain in his cage all day, alone and depressed? How would he handle the continued stress of being housed in a room of cats meowing their misery?* If the bunny's needs weren't met, he'd die.

A staff member entered from the canine quarters, and the barking of eager dogs waiting to be adopted entered with him. The bunny flinched and tried to duck into the folds of my sweatshirt. That decided his fate: he was going home with me.

While completing adoption papers, I heard his story. A heartless human had discarded the baby rabbit in a garden after a dog attacked the tiny prey animal. An elderly man rescued the injured baby from a bed of tulips and rushed him to the Denver facility, where emergency veterinary treatment prevented the rabbit's death from shock.

Courtney McCarty Johnson

After his wounds were cleaned and stitched, the handsome bunny was put into a cage in the only place available—a room filled with caged and distressed cats. After that the young bunny was basically ignored because staff members were unfamiliar with the temperament, behaviors, and needs of rabbits.

Tulip, named for the flowers in which he'd been found, was delighted to accompany me home. He was even more excited to find he was going to live with a playmate, Benjamin Bunny. The two became bonded buddies without delay.

Tulip, still a baby, wasn't exhibiting his full personality yet, but I blithely assumed he'd be much like Benjamin Bunny, my "perfect little Dutch boy" who is sweet and quiet and prides himself on keeping his brown-and-white coat neatly groomed. Oh, how very wrong I was. And how illogical. Why would two distinct little beings have the same personality? Before long, Tulip began demonstrating his.

He nosed open the office door (I still don't know how he accomplished that) and chewed through the computer cables. Thankful the equipment was off and he hadn't been injured, I replaced cables and covered them with hard plastic conduit. Before I could complete the task, he'd severed the telephone connection. Then the stereo wires.

When I saw him eyeing baseboards, I smugly stayed one hop ahead and sprayed them with bitter apple—only to learn the taste was much to his liking. I had to do some "creative" decorating, the looks of which would never pass a house-beautiful test!

After Tulip was neutered, he seemed to settle down, and I succumbed to a false confidence. Until it was time to clean bookshelves. Without a second thought, I laid some of the volumes on the coffee table. Tulip climbed aboard and chewed the edges of my most valued book, a sentimental gift. He snubbed the inexpensive paperbacks.

I was really exasperated and completely dumbfounded. The rabbits had a nice supply of hard plastic toys, untreated wood blocks, and unsprayed, dried apple branches. Why wasn't Tulip chewing on those?

"Why can't you be more like Benjamin?" I heard myself grumble time and again.

My patience came to an end the day I heard a loud rip from behind the sofa. I ran over and looked behind it. There sat my dark-cheeked adolescent, covered with stuffing. He had the most innocent look on his little face, as if to say, "I don't know how this happened, Mom. That couch just blew this all over me!"

All my frustration and irritation came out in one vocal blast. Tulip's nut-brown eyes widened in fear, and he scurried to a hiding place.

I felt awful. I knew better than to yell at any animal, especially one as sensitive as a rabbit. But what was I going to do with Tulip? His ripping and gnawing were emptying my bank account. I was beginning to call him Pricey Tulip!

Then it hit me. The all-important rule when bringing a rabbit into one's home is *think like the rabbit*. Instead of "listening" to Tulip's needs through observation and analysis of his behaviors, I had assumed he'd outgrow his chewing habits and become like Benjamin Bunny. Not only did Tulip have the attribute of youth, which made him naturally a bit wild and unruly, but he had been striving to gain my attention in order to say he was *B O R E D!*

With my new awareness, I began shopping—bunny style. Within hours of returning home, the family room was transformed into a rabbit paradise. Cardboard tubes edged the sides of the couch. Boxes of various sizes and shapes, each with escape holes and all sturdy enough to jump on, added interest. The *pièce de résistance* was a plastic playset that had inclines and platforms. Secret passageways and a courtyard completed the rabbit kingdom.

Tulip didn't wait for me to finish. He immediately entered the tubes, his best friend close behind, and a spirited game of chase began. The two agile racers maneuvered the course, jumping and short-cutting their way around as they explored the new territory.

In a surprise move, Tulip ran over to me, jumped into my lap, and reached up to lick my face. A quick "thank you" (something he'd never done before), a brief rest, and he was off again.

Tulip has taught me well. Even though our rooms are completely bunny-proofed, I do not leave him to roam the house unattended. He's a rabbit who lives in anticipation of new adventures and challenges. And as I continue to think like a rabbit, I'm able to meet those challenges.

Tulip seems content with his life now. He and his buddy, Benjamin Bunny, have plenty of toys and untreated wood, and I reconfigure the play spaces often enough to keep their interest piqued.

I'm content now too. I have happy, healthy bunnies—a source of great joy. I have Tulip to thank for that. Precious and priceless, that's my Tulip!

ABOUT RABBITS: bunny-proofing the house

Rabbits present some unexpected challenges, especially when it comes to their natural instincts for chewing and digging. Sometimes it may seem that nothing is safe from a rabbit's teeth, or that a rabbit is going to dig through the carpeting, right down to the foundation of the house!

It's important to remember that chewing and digging are purely instinctive behaviors. A rabbit's need to chew is so strong that the instinct will eclipse any training to minimize it. To prevent injury or death to the rabbit and damage to the household, bunny-proofing is *essential*. Make things inaccessible, use deterrents, and furnish appealing alternatives for chewing and digging. Watch to see what attracts a bunny's attention and take preventive measures. Keep in mind the social nature of rabbits and provide companionship and play. (Note that before expecting a rabbit to be a cooperative member of the family, it is imperative that the bunny be spayed or neutered, litter-trained, and socialized.)

Effective bunny-proofing is a proactive state of mind. To stay at least one hop ahead, get down on the floor at rabbit-level and survey the world. Start thinking like a rabbit—specifically, think like *your* rabbit.

Brown Beauty

Information for this story was provided by R. Lee Terence

Some say Show Low, which acquired its name from the winning hand in a poker game, is simply a small rural community. Others say it's a vacation destination. One thing is certain: Show Low's location at the edge of the Mogollon Rim ranks it with some of the prettiest places in all of Arizona. But, as can happen anywhere on this old planet of ours, some days that beauty is marred, as it was one cold, gray, drizzly day in April.

Parking at a street corner, a man unloaded several boxes and placed them under the ponderosa pines. He opened them, then climbed back into his vehicle and drove off.

A concerned neighbor who observed the incident was the first to call. "Bunnies are running all over the place! Could be a dozen. Maybe more."

I didn't ask for many details. Frankly, I long ago passed needing to know the particulars. After years of working with organizations that rescue cats, dogs, horses, birds, and any other unfortunate animal that is abandoned, neglected, or abused, I've seen more than I ever wanted to see of what some call the dark side of human nature.

Domestic rabbits running loose could mean only one thing: someone had abandoned them.

I loaded the humane traps and sped along the highway. Two kind-hearted citizens anticipated my arrival and were waiting; they began talking before I got out of my truck.

"Roaming dogs got two of 'em!"

"One got hit by a car."

By this time, the bunnies, crazed with fear, had scattered. I looked around, noting the fact that the man who dumped them had chosen an area that had a bit of underbrush, an overturned boat or two, and some resident vehicles. At least the defenseless animals had a few places to hide.

I had to hurry; frenzied barking meant the dogs had probably killed a third. The two compassionate residents helped me set up live-catch traps, and from then on, it was a waiting game.

Turns out we didn't have to wait long: two emaciated rabbits bolted eagerly into traps to devour the cilantro. Two, then four, were moved to safety. A couple of hours passed; we captured another, and then my helpers had to head for home.

I was alone, and patience and worry sat side-by-side on my shoulders. The clouded sun was setting, and the tall pines made nightfall even darker.

I was sure two bunnies were still alive. Thinking parsley might tempt them, I used some to bait the traps, all the while keeping an eye on the dogs eagerly scouting the area. I was luckier than the dogs; hunger finally got the best of both rabbits and they willingly allowed themselves to be snagged.

While transferring the last rabbits to carriers, I spotted a skinny, unkempt, brownish-colored bunny watching from the sidelines. It looked as if she might be injured.

I readied a trap and stationed myself to watch. The scrawny rabbit's swift motion took me by surprise: she raced in, snatched the offered fare, turned tail, and disappeared! I arranged more tempting sprigs, this time further back. The same thing happened. She was hurt but smart; she'd figured out how to pull out the food without engaging the trap door.

Cold as it was, I was determined to get this plain little girl, whom most would overlook in favor of some exotic-looking rabbit. I just hoped I could catch her before some predator did.

But my luck ran out. Daylight disappeared, the rabbit along with it. It was almost inky out there; the clouds had settled low, cloaking the tops of the ponderosas. I knew better than to use one of my high-powered flashlights—that would've done more harm than good.

I hoped the bunny was in hiding and sent a mental message that she should stay put. Fastening a big bundle of greens as far back as possible, I made sure she'd have to really work to get any, then covered the trap with my heavy canvas tarp and secured everything tight against the wind. A flapping, noisy thing would certainly scare that rabbit away.

When it was obvious there was nothing more I could do, I sent out a little prayer and went home.

Just after dawn, I checked the trap. There she was, sitting inside, her stand-up ears perked forward, with a look that said, "WHAT TOOK YOU SO LONG?"

The dingy-brown bunny obligingly let me put her in a carrier. Once home, the amiable little one let me inspect her dog bites and care for the wounds. Then she ate her first nourishing meal in a long while, maybe the first one ever. She was so unbelievably thin; the sparse coat of dirty fur couldn't hide the sharp feel of her backbone or the obvious edges of her ribs. There were scrapes and tears in her skin. She wouldn't have lived much longer.

The veterinarian guessed the rabbit was just over a year old. She weighed four pounds, about half what she should have. As soon as she was healthy enough, I was going to have her spayed by a vet who was skilled in treating rabbits. I'd already contacted Brambley Hedge Rabbit Rescue about that.

Brown Beauty is what I called her, Beauty for short. I thought it was a fitting name for a rabbit who had an inner strength and sweetness that surpassed many of my acquaintance. She was outgoing, yet gentle. And she didn't mind being picked up, an unusual trait in most rabbits, but especially amazing in one so obviously neglected. As Beauty regained strength and her wounds began to heal, she started running around the house and had a grand time finding out-of-the-way places to hide. She was always glad to see me, though, and would come when called.

Three weeks after she was trapped, just before she was to be spayed, Beauty began stuffing her mouth with impossible amounts of hay and frantically racing around the living room. She emptied the contents of her mouth and worked that hay around with her nose, then grabbed it up and ran to another place.

I'd never seen anything like this before. A call to Brambley Hedge brought me up short: Beauty was trying to find a place to build a nest! She was such a skinny little thing that I hadn't considered that she might've been pregnant when I trapped her. I wondered if it could be a false pregnancy. I hoped so, but wasn't going to bet on it.

Well, if Brown Beauty was going to deliver, she'd need a cozy box. I gave her one I thought would work. Sure enough, she finally decided that was where she'd build the nest. After forming a circular depression in the hay, Beauty pulled fur from her breast and made a warm, downy bed for her babies. I'd found out that when a doe is about to deliver, the fur on her chest loosens, providing soft nesting material and exposing her nipples for nursing.

After all that, Beauty lay quietly, as if tired by her work. Just before bed, I peeked in on her; she was squatting over the nest. Worried that she might leave droppings there, I stuck around to clean up. But a short time later, when Beauty eased herself away, there were two tiny pink babies. Five more followed. A couple of days later, enough fur had grown on their naked bodies for me to see their individual colors: black, gray, tan, brown, and one blond runt.

After what Beauty had endured, it seemed miraculous she could deliver seven perfect babies.

In typical human fashion, I accepted the miracle, then started worrying. *Would Beauty be able to care for her tiny, blind dependents? What if she was too stressed to produce milk? What if she deserted them?*

At first, I thought my fears had been realized. Beauty covered her brood with fur and hay, hopped away, and lay down as far from them as she could get. I moved her close to her kits, hoping she'd take an interest in them, but she snorted and returned to where she had been. Finally, I called Brambley Hedge again and learned that mother rabbits stay away from their odorless babies so as not to attract predators. I was assured that Beauty most likely would take care of her babies during the night; I sure hoped so. It was a long, fitful night for me.

The next morning, there she was, just where I had left her the night before. I lifted a bit of hay and fur off the nest and was relieved to find all the babies had round little bellies and unwrinkled skin. They'd been fed.

For days, I never saw Beauty approach her offspring, but they were always clean and well fed when I peered in on them.

It occurred to me what a privilege it was to observe Beauty, one of the prettiest rabbits around, exhibiting such pure love. Confidently and single-mindedly, she gave herself to her little ones. In her sweet, unassuming way, she nurtured her babies, treating them all as the perfect little beings they were. To me, that's beauty by any name.

ABOUT RABBITS: benefits of spaying and neutering

It is obvious that spaying and neutering reduce rabbit overpopulation and its resulting horrors (neglect, abandonment, and euthanasia). Less well known, perhaps, is the fact that "fixing" also helps to:

- accomplish litter box training with respect to urine (it *cannot* be accomplished if the bunny is unaltered)
- reduce hormonally driven aggression and grouchiness
- eliminate territorial spraying
- decrease the chances of a female rabbit's dying of uterine cancer.

For the comfort, health, and well-being of your rabbits, have them spayed or neutered by a veterinarian experienced in treating rabbits. Most vets prefer to spay a healthy female when she is between 4 and 6 months of age. Performing a good spay before that age is technically difficult and may result in retained tissue, which can produce hormones throughout the rabbit's life and result in behavior problems. In addition, anesthesia poses greater risks for small and/or young animals.

Healthy male rabbits can be neutered after their testicles descend. The testicles of small and average-size males may drop down as early as 10 weeks of age and almost always by the age of 3-1/2 months, while the testicles of giant breeds may not be evident until the age of 8 months.

Human guardians should become aware of the factors and variables that affect sexual maturity and must separate male and female bunnies at the age of 10 weeks to prevent unwanted litters.

Drowned Rats

by Nancy LaRoche

I had just sat down to what was supposed to be my first leisurely breakfast that week when the phone rang. Envisioning my meal growing cold while someone chattered at me, I reluctantly answered.

To my surprise, the caller was Georgia, who along with her partner Steve operated Willow Run, one of the feed stores in our Colorado community. Her voice, usually low and calm, was uncharacteristically high-pitched.

"... left them in a box, and I don't know what to do," she cried into the phone. "They're wet and cold, and I think some are dead. Can you come?" I'd missed the beginning of the first sentence, but the panic in her voice sent me into high gear.

"Coming!" I cried and dropped the receiver into its cradle. Grabbing the keys, I ran to my car.

I was surprised by a cold, early spring sleet that had begun during the night. It quickly wet my shirt and pricked my arms with icy needles. But remembering the urgency in Georgia's voice, I didn't return for a jacket.

Five minutes later, I was shivering in the big, barn-like building that housed Willow Run's packaged goods. Georgia, a square-built woman, was kneeling over a wet cardboard box on the floor, dabbing a towel at some small dark lumps inside it. Instead of the tough-as-nails businesswoman that most people knew, she was now an "anxious mother," her usual response to an animal in distress.

This morning, fury animated her wide face. Looking up at me, she choked out, "Someone left them in this box outside the door. When the sleet began, it soaked them. I think they're hypothermic." Her voice shook with anger. Then, with fear creeping into her tone, she stated simply, "I don't know what to do."

The five cold, wet lumps that lay there were hardly bigger than the one in my throat and, like it, seemed frozen in place. Two of them kicked spasmodically, indicating the possibility of life, but in a manner that more strongly suggested the throes of death. *Drowned rats* was the phrase that popped into my head, but they were neither drowned (I hoped) nor rats. The tiny elongated ears that lay plastered to their shoulders indicated clearly that the icy blobs were baby bunnies.

For a moment, I was overwhelmed with horror and despair. *How could people abandon baby bunnies like this? Had they bought two rabbits and been assured that both were females, only to discover otherwise when a litter arrived? Or had they bought a single rabbit, not knowing she was already pregnant? Or maybe they had wanted their children to see the "miracle of birth," but hadn't wanted to take responsibility for the results of that birth.*

Since beginning my rabbit-rescue work, I had discovered that many unwanted rabbits come into the world in these ways, only to be abandoned. But I couldn't fathom how anyone could dump so much responsibility on someone else's doorstep or fail to care enough to assure the survival of the bunnies until someone found them.

Staring at the disaster before me, I felt hopelessly inadequate. I had so little experience. Most of what I knew about rabbits came from books. I'd worked with rabbits at the Humane Society of Boulder Valley, but none of my limited skills prepared me for a situation like this.

The subconscious, though, is a mysterious thing. It sometimes whispers to our conscious mind what we need to know in a given situation. Such was the case this day.

"Georgia, is the grooming room open?" I asked.

Without answering, Georgia grabbed a key from under the counter and unlocked the door to that room. I began running warm water into the sink. Hands shaking with fear and hope, I quickly immersed one of the blobs of wet fur and cold flesh, keeping the head above water, and gently massaged the small, plump body. The sudden, purposeful wiggling I felt as the tiny bit of bunny warmed was like a miracle. Georgia had already turned on the drying cage. I toweled the bunny and transferred him, or perhaps her, into it.

Three more times, I immersed and tenderly kneaded the small bodies. Georgia toweled them. Incredibly, four miniature white-and-gray fluff balls were now happily preening themselves in the warmth of the dryer, as if they'd just wakened from a nap and needed to put a few hairs back in place. Short forelegs stretched to clean adorable little faces, able to reach only the chins and whiskers. Tiny feet pulled delicate, upright ears down to be carefully cleaned by pink tongues. Bright, alert eyes gazed at us all the while. Their expressions looking at us were very much like ours looking at them—expressions that might be interpreted as, "How fascinating you are!"

Twisting to one side and then the other, the baby rabbits shifted their efforts from faces to backs and sides. Then they stretched improbably long hind legs forward, spreading their toes while busily grooming each one. When finished, the bunnies seemed to pause for a moment, as if contemplating what to do next.

Suddenly, one bunny shot unexpectedly into the air, as if a spring had been released beneath him. Then another popped. Soon all four were leaping and falling over each other, expressing the joy of life in which rabbits seem to specialize.

Sadly, the fifth bunny was another story. I had immersed him and massaged, but there had been no answering wiggles, only a tiny spasm and then a small limp body, lifeless on a towel. Tears blinded me as I dried him, inwardly cursing my helplessness to do anything more than to restore a bit of fluffiness to his reddish-brown coat.

Four were alive and apparently well, but I keenly felt the loss of this fifth one. Had the five been stuffed toy animals, losing one wouldn't have mattered so much. But this had been a sentient being, endowed with the same desire to live and the same abilities to think and feel that are shared by all animals. He was important as an individual and the survival of his siblings didn't lessen the loss of *him*.

Fluffing his coat, I wondered about my need to do so. Was I trying to disguise death? Was it an apology for my inability to catch that last spark of life and fan it into a flame? Perhaps it was nothing more than an expression of sorrow.

"I'm so sorry, little one," I whispered. "So very, very sorry."

As I turned back, seeking comfort in the sight of the cute, living bunnies, Steve came in to check on how things were going. He'd seen the box with its miserable contents and was anxious to know whether our efforts had been

successful. Observing the four, he said, "Well, four out of five isn't bad." And then he looked at the little body on the counter where I had left it and added, "But five out of five is great!"

For an instant, the significance of his last words failed to register. Then my gaze whipped to the little body on the counter—there, before my amazed eyes, the tiny creature was struggling to his feet. A surge of gratitude for a life returned swept over me. Breathless with wonder, I put him with his siblings, where he joined them in their grooming rituals.

When the bunnies were fully dry, Georgia turned off the drying cage and fetched a dish of pellets, alfalfa hay, and a low crock of water, placing all on the floor within easy reach of the bunnies. They nibbled hungrily while we watched in rapt delight. Tummies full, they tumbled together, each struggling to bury him- or herself beneath the others. A few moments later, there was only a soft pile of fur, with a couple of unexpected ears and legs sticking out at random angles, motionless except for a gentle rise and fall indicating sound sleep.

My elation was inexpressible. Georgia's and Steve's beaming faces and the sight of five healthy bunnies made me feel like some sort of miracle worker. Few things I'd done in my life seemed as meaningful as helping these furry little babies return to playing, eating, and sleeping, as if it were just another day in their young lives.

Which, thankfully, it was.

ABOUT RABBITS: keeping a bunny clean

Although warm water was used as an emergency measure in this story, as a general rule a rabbit should never be bathed. The experience is so stressful that a bunny is likely to become ill. In addition, a rabbit who gets wet to the skin becomes easily chilled and can go into shock, which can be lethal. The only way to ensure a rabbit is completely dry is to use a professional drying cage, as was done for the baby bunnies in this story.

If a bunny cannot groom herself, the caregiver can help by lifting the fur with one hand, then gently combing the fine hairs out from under that hand with a comb. In the event a rabbit is soiled with feces, some fur may need to be cut off—but extreme care must be taken so that the rabbit's skin is not lifted into the path of the scissors or electric shears. If a rabbit is soiled with urine, it may be necessary to spot wash a small area, maintaining the rabbit in a warm space until she is completely dry. A soft towel dampened with vinegar will help alleviate urine odor, but the stain will remain until the rabbit molts and grows new fur.

Velly Oliver

AFTERWORD
So You're Thinking about Getting a Rabbit. . .

Rabbits are full of personality and *joie de vivre!* After reading about how much fun they are, you may think that living with a house rabbit is something you'd like to try.

STOP! Don't act on impulse. Though living with companion rabbits can be a terrific experience, they require a big investment in time, attention, and special care. Because of their physical construction and prey mentality, rabbits are very different from the cats and dogs with whom so many of us share our lives.

Before bringing a bunny home, do some serious research. Then think it over and be honest with yourself whether you can commit to meeting all of a rabbit's needs, including the expense. Rabbits are wonderful animals, but they do not fit into every lifestyle.

Love Your Rabbit
The Basics of Rabbit Care

Companionship   Rabbits are very social creatures; they need friends and playtime. They are most active at dawn and dusk and generally take a deep mid-day nap, so activities should generally correspond to the bunnies' natural schedule.

Human guardian   Adults must assume full responsibility for the rabbits' care and safety. An attentive caregiver understands and appreciates the independent nature and prey responses of rabbits.

Veterinarian   A vet who is knowledgeable about rabbits is essential, and back-up emergency care is just as important.

Spay/neuter   "Altering" a rabbit reduces health risks, results in fewer behavior problems, and stops the cycle of overpopulation. Vets generally prefer to spay or neuter rabbits at 4-6 months of age, but the actual timing is breed-dependent. Because rabbits can reach sexual maturity as early as 2-1/2 months, males and females should be kept separated from the age of 10 weeks until they can be altered by a vet experienced in treating rabbits.

Proper diet and fresh water   Diet must be based on the age of the rabbit. Grass hay, properly balanced pellets, selected vegetables (if the rabbit is old enough and can tolerate them), and fresh water must be provided daily.

Bunny-proofing	This is essential for the safety of the rabbit and to prevent damage to your home. Don't rely on training alone, and never assume a rabbit's lack of interest in an item means she will always avoid that object.
Socialization	In addition to establishing a good relationship with a rabbit for the fun of interacting with him, it's critical that the human caretaker be able to pick up the bunny for grooming and in the event of a health problem. A rabbit must be handled gently and correctly to prevent injury.
Housing	A rabbit's home should be large enough so he can stand up, stretch out, and move about; there also needs to be room for an appropriately-sized litter box. Solid flooring (not wire) must be available in at least a portion of the condo.
Location of home	Safety and social interaction are important. The condo should be located away from drafts, heat, and high-pitched and/or loud noises, but situated so the rabbit can observe family interactions.
Cleanliness of home	Clean the condo when the rabbits are outside of it. A solution of vinegar and water is safest; rinse well, then dry.
Litter box	The box should be sized to the rabbit. Paper litters or wood stove pellets are good. Don't use clay or aromatic litters (e.g., cedar shavings) or materials that rabbits will eat (e.g., wheat and corn litters).
Play spaces	Be creative! Rabbits love tubes, low ramps, and boxes with holes cut into them. Change the configuration to pique interest.
Items for chewing and digging	Observe what attracts your rabbit's attention. In addition to grass hay, provide such things as grass mats and untreated wood that is nontoxic and resin-free (e.g., unsprayed, dried apple branches). Make a digging box: a covered box with a hole cut into the side, filled with paper litter.

Bunnies + Classrooms = *Mismatch!*

The following article was written because of Kali, the rabbit who inspired this book. She was born in a preschool classroom, removed too young from her mother, put alone into a cage in a different classroom, and then not given proper care. It is my hope that this article will educate parents and teachers and will prevent such misfortune from befalling another hapless bunny.

The classroom is abuzz with afternoon activity. In one corner, a small group of children reads aloud the simple stories they've written. Across the room, another cluster claps out the rhythms to a poem. A quartet chants the addition tables. Two youngsters push bits of crackers into the cage of the classroom bunny. Through the open window comes the sound of a whistle, starting the gym relay.

From the bunny's perspective, what's wrong with this picture?

Just about everything!

"Mismatch" means *to match unsuitably or inaccurately*, and classrooms (including preschool rooms) happen to be very unsuitable "homes" for rabbits. *Why?* A few facts may help explain.

- Rabbits have been domesticated for a relatively short period of time, and they retain many of the instincts of the European wild rabbits from whom they descended. For example, they instinctively seek shelter and sleep during the day to avoid predators and midday heat (even when safety and high temperatures are not a concern), and they innately dig and chew.

- Rabbits are prey animals. Dogs and cats, the companion animals with whom most of us are familiar, are predators. If traits and behaviors of dogs and cats are projected onto rabbits, misunderstandings and misconceptions about rabbits and their behaviors result.

- Rabbits are culturally viewed as sweet, cuddly, gentle pets. Although this is certainly part of their nature, in other respects they are quite the opposite: independent and strong-willed, feisty and territorial, and sometimes aggressive or grouchy (especially if not neutered or spayed).

- Rabbits' chewing behavior, which some people view solely as destructive, is spurred by physiology. Their teeth, which grow continuously throughout life, are made for chewing fibrous, coarse, and abrasive plant materials, such as grass hay. The action of the teeth grinding together as tough plant materials are consumed helps maintain the proper length and shape of the teeth. Both proper diet and veterinary care are critical for preventing the health issues that can result from tooth overgrowth.

Here are some of the ways in which the needs of rabbits and the needs of children diverge, creating a definite mismatch.

- Rabbits are crepuscular, a zoological reference to being naturally active before sunrise and at twilight.
  Children (and most teachers) are generally out of the classroom during those times, depriving the resident bunny of the opportunities to interact socially and to exercise outside the cage during his normal active time.

- Rabbits instinctively take a deep nap during the middle of the day and are easily stressed by noise and commotion when they need to sleep.
  Healthy, happy kids are active and boisterous and are often allowed to interact with the rabbit during the bunny's natural quiet time.

- Rabbits need a safe, open exercise space.
  Most classrooms are not bunny-proofed, which can result in damage to the room—and injury or death to the rabbit. Desks, tables, cabinets, and bookcases allow only minimal exercise space and pose potential safety concerns for a free-roaming rabbit. In addition, the bunny can be accidentally sat on, kicked, or stepped on as adults and children move about the room.

- Rabbits, as prey animals, instinctively seek their safe place and are often territorial about their home.
  Children want to show their love and attention by trying to pet the bunny and often stick their finger,

pencil, or other object through the wire sides of the cage. Such actions are very stressful and unsafe for a rabbit—and unsafe for the children, as a rabbit may lunge and bite as a means of defense.

- Rabbits need a regular routine and predictable surroundings.

  Children proudly take the bunny home for a weekend, not realizing how frightening the strange noises, odors, activities, other household animals, and unfamiliar routines are to a rabbit. Separating two rabbits who live together in the classroom and sending each one home to a different family creates incredible stress for the bunnies. However, leaving a rabbit alone in the classroom for a weekend or holiday puts the rabbit in jeopardy, since these delicate creatures must be cared for and monitored on a daily basis.

- Rabbits instinctively hide symptoms of illness or injury.

  It's easy for a busy teacher or classroom aide to miss the subtle, but critical, signs of illness in a rabbit. Sending a bunny home with students for weekends, holidays, or vacation can result in symptoms of serious illness being overlooked or ignored. If there are other pets in the home, the rabbit may be exposed to certain trans-species illnesses.

- Rabbits are considered "exotics" in veterinary terminology, and they need regular check-ups by vets who know rabbits well.

  It's incumbent upon the teacher to obtain proper medical care for a classroom rabbit. School district funds aren't generally allocated for animal care, which places the financial burden on the teacher. If the rabbit's health needs are not met, children may inadvertently learn that it's okay to have animals even if one can't properly care for them.

- Rabbits have fragile bodies and must be handled carefully.

  Youngsters are very eager, do not know their own strength, and often don't respect a rabbit's needs. A child tends to grab and hold a bunny improperly and too tightly.

- Rabbits have delicate, complex digestive systems and may become ill, and even die, from eating the wrong foods.

  Children are frequently allowed to feed bunnies foods that the teacher may not realize are inappropriate. In an attempt to be "friends," a child might sneak forbidden/toxic foods or too many treats to the rabbit.

- Rabbits require a quality high-fiber diet, and grass hay should be available at all times. Pellets and/or specific fresh vegetables are daily necessities, based on the bunny's age, weight, and health.

  Hay creates a mess, poses storage problems, and may trigger allergies in some children and adults. Fresh vegetables require refrigeration. Inappropriate vegetables—or any vegetables fed to a very young rabbit—can cause illness or death.

- Rabbits groom their fur regularly, although some breeds, especially those with long hair, need assistance.

  Proper grooming of a long-haired rabbit is time-consuming and should occur daily when the rabbit is shedding and at least weekly during the rest of the year. Children and adults may have allergic reactions to rabbit fur.

- Rabbits are intelligent, inquisitive, social beings who need stimulation, freedom, and lots of interaction during their active time.

  Most teachers' main focus is, understandably, on the students—not on keeping a classroom rabbit challenged and stimulated. No one may notice that the isolated bunny is lonely and depressed.

Before bringing a rabbit (or guinea pig, hamster, or other animal) into the classroom, a teacher should honestly ask him- or herself: Why do I want a bunny in the classroom? What exactly am I using him to teach?

It may be that the teacher wishes to model responsible behavior or to provide an experience for children who, for various reasons, don't have a companion animal at home. Or perhaps the instructor wants students to research rabbits, then apply that learning to other topics. Sometimes the true answer may be that the rabbit isn't really for teaching purposes, but rather for entertainment or novelty in the classroom.

In all cases, there is a need for a sincere answer to an additional question: Can I ensure that *all* the needs of the rabbit—a high maintenance pet—will be properly met? In most situations, the answer will be "no" and alternative teaching solutions should be found.

There is another pivotal issue that concerns the welfare of rabbits (and other classroom pets) at the end of a semester or school year. Often the classroom bunny is joyously passed along to a student's family, who may know nothing about the care or needs of a rabbit. If the situation doesn't work out, the well-meaning family may hope the bunny finds a new home through the local animal shelter or may even harbor the common misconception that domesticated rabbits can survive in the wild. Animal rescue organizations receive calls during the school year regarding classroom bunnies needing a home.

Therefore, a teacher should also address the following: If the rabbit has to be relinquished for *any* reason, what will happen to him? For example, what will happen to the bunny at the end of the semester or school year or if I should happen to leave my teaching position? What if someone in the classroom is allergic to the bunny's fur or to the hay? What will I do if a student is not gentle enough to be safely near the bunny or if the frightened rabbit bites a child? Am I willing to give the bunny a permanent, loving home to ensure he doesn't end up an unwanted rabbit, consigned to a hutch, taken to a shelter (where he may be euthanized), or released into the wild (where he will die unless rescued)?

Bunnies and classrooms are a serious mismatch because the nature and requirements of a rabbit and the realities and needs of students are fundamentally incompatible. In contrast, a rabbit will thrive in a home that honors her needs for affection, health, safety, and free expression of her multifaceted nature.

Finding Quality Veterinary Care for Your Rabbit

by Lucile C. Moore

Even the best-cared-for rabbits become injured or ill or develop other conditions requiring veterinary care.

- When a rabbit requires medical care, time is critical. A rabbit's inability to tolerate pain can lead to life-threatening digestive complications. (The digestive system is the first thing to shut down when a rabbit suffers physical and/or emotional stress.)
- Your primary veterinarian may not always be available due to vacations, off-hours, conferences, illness, or family concerns. It is important to locate a back-up vet *before* an emergency arises.
- The length of your rabbit's life may depend upon the quality of the primary and back-up veterinary care you find.

Keep these things in mind when searching for a good rabbit veterinarian:

- If you already have a vet who is excellent with your cat or dog, don't assume he or she will be just as good with your rabbit.
- From a medical standpoint, rabbits are considered "exotics." However, a veterinarian listing "exotics" may be knowledgeable about birds or reptiles yet know little or nothing about treating rabbits.
- Just because a veterinarian *claims* to be a good rabbit vet does not necessarily mean it is true.

- Ideally, the location of both your primary and back-up veterinary practices should be near enough that you can have your rabbit there within 30-45 minutes in an emergency.

Begin your search for a rabbit vet by making a list of possibilities.
- Ask friends with rabbits what veterinarians they use and why.
- Call your local rabbit rescue organization to ask what veterinarians they recommend. Or check the vet listing at http://www.morfz.com and the list of recommended veterinarians maintained by the House Rabbit Society at http://www.rabbit.org/vets.
- Speak to the office personnel of veterinarians in your area and ask if any vets in the practice treat rabbits and, if so, how many they see in an average week. (Comparing the numbers will give you an idea as to where most people take their rabbits for treatment.)
- Put the names of the veterinarians who come up most frequently on your short list.

Make appointments to speak to the veterinarians on your short list (either in person or on the telephone) and ask questions to determine their understanding of rabbits and rabbit medicine.
- Do you routinely prescribe pain medication for ill, injured, and post-operative rabbits? (Rabbits do not tolerate pain well and need to be kept pain-free to aid recovery.)
- What antibiotics are unsafe for rabbits? (e.g., amoxicillin, lincomycin, clindamycin, ampicillin, erythromycin, tilmicosin)
- Whenever possible, are you willing to allow a rabbit to return home the same day after treatment or an operation? (Rabbits are often stressed unnecessarily by being left at a veterinary clinic overnight.)
- Do you recommend fasting a rabbit (withholding food and water) before surgical procedures? (This is not necessary for rabbits and can lead to serious digestive complications. The one exception is abdominal surgery, when food may be withheld for *only* an hour or two.)
- How many rabbit spays have you performed?
- What teaching hospital or consultant do you contact when you have questions regarding a difficult rabbit case? (If a veterinarian does not have a prompt response to this question, it could indicate a lack of willingness to seek expert advice when needed.)

If taking these steps fails to lead you to good primary and back-up rabbit veterinarians (not uncommon in small towns or rural areas), you will need to modify your search.

- Look for a veterinarian who treats a wide variety of animal species, such as a country vet who treats everything from cattle to cats.
- A vet with the self-confidence to admit when he/she does not know something and who asks questions is often better than one who feels he/she must always have an answer.
- Ask if the veterinarian attends any professional conferences and if he/she would be willing to attend presentations on rabbits at those conferences. (Veterinarians who keep up on the latest developments in veterinary medicine will more likely be willing to expand their patient base and learn to treat new species.)

Educate yourself. Learn the signs of both healthy and ailing rabbits so you will know when to call the veterinarian and what to do for your rabbit until you can reach medical help.

- Purchase several good books on house rabbit care and know the symptoms of stress, injury, and illness.
- Read Kathy Smith's article, titled "Rabbit Health: Should I Be Worried?" available in the December 2004 archives at http://mysweetpet.com/ (click on "Archives") as well as articles by Dana Krempels at http://www.bio.miami.edu/hare/rabbithealth.html.
- Buy or create a basic first aid kit for rabbits and know how to use it.
- Receive instruction from your vet before administering medications or performing medical/dental procedures on your rabbit.
- Invest in at least one veterinary text about rabbits for detailed physiological information and for emergency reference.
- Keep up with the latest developments in rabbit care and medicine by regularly accessing a reliable website such as http://www.medirabbit.com, http://www.rabbit.org, or http://www.morfz.com.

Rabbit Teeth:
The Importance of Proper Care

by Angela M. Lennox, DVM Dipl. ABVP-Avian
President of the Association of Exotic Mammal Veterinarians

Some of the stories in this book are about rabbits who suffered such cruel neglect that their deaths were imminent. In two accounts, people skilled in caring for rabbits provided emergency measures, including clipping the incisors. Because the teeth affect a variety of health issues and also because some individuals may be tempted to perform at-home care, here is a short overview of rabbit dentition.

The most unique feature of rabbit teeth is that both the incisors (front teeth) and the molars (cheek teeth) grow continually throughout the life of the rabbit. Maintaining the normal length and shape of these ever-growing teeth is accomplished in healthy rabbits as the teeth grind against each other, especially when crushing very fibrous plant materials like grass hay. Although the causes of molar overgrowth and uneven growth are not definitive, lack of fiber (hay) in the diet is almost certainly a factor.

When molars wear unevenly and overgrow, chewing puts excessive pressure on the roots. The resulting damage can predispose the tooth to fracture and abscess. Diseased teeth often bend and grow in abnormal directions, which can result in damage to soft tissues, including the tongue and cheeks. All these dental disorders cause significant pain, weight loss, and debilitation.

Overgrowth of the incisors can be caused by congenital malformation of the jaw (especially in rabbits bred for shortened facial structure, such as lop and dwarf breeds) or by overgrowth of the cheek teeth. Elongated incisors generally grow in abnormal directions, causing soft tissue injury, pain, and impaired ability to eat.

In cases of congenital jaw malformation, extraction of the incisors is often the best treatment. Rabbits without incisors generally do very well, moving the food with their lips and tongue to the back of the mouth and then chewing it with their molars.

Dental disease is a serious health issue and must be treated by a veterinarian skilled in this area of rabbit medicine and surgery. The small size of a rabbit's mouth and the presence of cheek folds limit the examination of all the molars, and sedation is frequently necessary. Veterinarians experienced in treating rabbits use specialized equipment to examine teeth and treat disorders, including high-speed dental burrs to shorten and shape the teeth. Simply clipping overgrown teeth with nail clippers or rongeurs carries a high risk of tooth fracture and abscess, does not allow teeth to be restored to normal shape, and does not address underlying issues such as infection.

Rabbits are complex little beings, and their health issues are very different from those of cats and dogs. Therefore, finding a qualified vet to treat your rabbit is of paramount importance. The Association of Exotic Mammal Veterinarians (AEMV) is working with the American Board of Veterinary Practitioners (ABVP) to establish an Exotic Companion Mammal Specialty. By 2008, exotic practitioners who apply for and successfully pass the rigorous testing process will be able to distinguish themselves as "rabbit specialists." For additional information, go to http://www.abvp.com and http://www.aemv.org.

Special Thanks

Authors

MICHAEL W. FOX, DSc, PhD, BVetMed, MRCVS, contributed the Foreword to this book. A veterinarian, bioethicist, conservationist, and lecturer, Dr. Fox is well known as the leader of the movement to foster the ethical treatment of animals. Prior to his retirement from The Humane Society of the United States in 2001, he held various positions with that organization, including senior scholar of bioethics, vice president, and director of the Center for Respect of Life and Environment. Dr. Fox is the syndicated columnist of "Animal Doctor," published weekly in newspapers across the US. A frequent guest on national television and radio network shows, Dr. Fox has authored more than 40 books. They encompass a wide scope of work, from the behavior of wild canids to understanding dogs and cats and from animal care to bioethics. His works include: *The Soul of the Wolf, Understanding Your Cat, Understanding Your Dog, The Healing Touch for Dogs/The Healing Touch for Cats, The Boundless Circle, Eating with Conscience,* and *Killer Foods.*

ANGELA M. LENNOX, DVM Dipl. ABVP-Avian, (contributor of "Rabbit Teeth: The Importance of Proper Care") has practiced exotic animal medicine exclusively for more than 15 years. As an adjunct professor at Purdue University School of Veterinary Medicine, she teaches a variety of topics in exotic animal medicine and surgery, as well as presenting at conferences and lecturing internationally. Dr. Lennox is editor of the *Rabbit and Rodent Dentistry Handbook.* Her articles have been published in various journals, including *Veterinary Clinics of North America: Avian and Exotic Practice, Seminars in Exotic Pet Medicine, Journal of Exotic Pet Medicine,* and *ExoticDVM.* Dr. Lennox is president of the Association of Exotic Mammal Veterinarians (http://www.aemv.org), an organization dedicated to improving the standards of exotic mammal medicine and surgery.

SUSAN CHERNAK MCELROY ("Emily") is a well-known speaker, facilitator, and best-selling author. Her books include *Animals as Teachers and Healers, Animals as Guides for the Soul, Heart in the Wild, All My Relations,* and *Why Buffalo Dance.* Her writing is also featured in many of the *Chicken Soup* volumes and in several anthologies, including *Kinship with the Animals, Wounded Healers,* and *Intimate Nature: The Bond between Woman and Animals.* Susan's life work is deeply influenced by her enchantment with and love of animals and nature, her personal experience with cancer, and her studies in indigenous traditions. For more information about Susan and her work, please visit her website at http://www.susanchernakmcelroy.com.

Lucile C. Moore ("Finding Quality Veterinary Care for Your Rabbit") is the author of *A House Rabbit Primer.* Her articles about rabbits have appeared online and in publications such as *Rabbits U.S.A.,* and she has served as a guest expert on nationally syndicated radio shows. Lucile has been rescuing animals all her life and has been working since 1994 to better the lives of companion rabbits.

Bernie S. Siegel, MD, ("Born to Be *ME!*") previously wrote *Smudge Bunny* (illustrated by Laura J. Bryant), a children's version of Smudge's story, and he and Smudge write animal-oriented articles for the quarterly *laJoie Journal.* Dr. Siegel's best sellers include *Love, Medicine & Miracles; Peace, Love & Healing; How to Live between Office Visits; Prescriptions for Living; Help Me to Heal; 365 Prescriptions for the Soul; 101 Exercises for the Soul;* and *Love, Magic & Mudpies.* A retired surgeon, Dr. Siegel developed the Exceptional Cancer Patients therapy program, an integrative approach to cancer that utilizes art, dreams, images, and feelings to bring about changes in an individual's life. For more information, visit Dr. Siegel's website at http://www.berniesiegelmd.com.

Artists

Susanna Dee created illustrations used in the front- and backmatter of the book. Susanna has been drawing ever since she can remember, receiving inspiration from nature and her family. While she works primarily in pencil, charcoal, and ink, her realistic style translates well into a variety of media. Susanna lives in California with her husband, children, cats, dogs, and fish. Visit her website at http://www.SusannaDee.com.

Beverly Endsley created illustrations for "Brown Beauty" (based on a description from R. Lee Terence), "Drowned Rats" (based on photos provided by Nancy LaRoche and O. Earl McCullough), and "Emily" (based on a photograph provided by Susan Chernak McElroy). An award-winning artist, Beverly is inspired by the old masters and uses techniques and paint preparations popular in Rembrandt's era. She especially enjoys the contrast of light and shadow (chiaroscuro). Beverly works in oil or watercolor to create wildlife paintings, portraits, and still lifes; her work also includes conté sketches. She lives with her husband and their furred family members in Evergreen, Colorado. Visit her website at http://www.beverlyendsley.com.

ANDI KLEINMAN created illustrations for "A Real Head-Turner" (based on photographs provided by Patrice Pruitte), "Born to Be *ME!*" (based on photographs provided by Dr. Bernie Siegel), "Frankie's Foible" (based on a description and photograph provided by Bea LeNoir), and for the chapter title pages. Andi's professional art career spans illustration, advertising, and graphic design for groups ranging from Babbitts Department Stores and Flagstaff Dark Skies Coalition to the USDA Forest Service. She enjoys playing with pencil, pen-and-ink, 3D mixed media, and fabric sculpture; her award-winning art dolls are made of recycled materials. Andi and her family live in Flagstaff, Arizona.

MARY ELLEN WEHRLI created illustrations for "Bunny's Christmas Kingdom: Joy Uncaged" and "The Day Bunny Stole the Game" (both based on photographs provided by Kimberly Dezelon), "Lobo and Blueberry" (based on photographs provided by Kay Fritzsche), and "Lovable Bobka" (based on photographs provided by Lena Sullivan). Mary Ellen has won awards for both abstract and representational paintings, and her work is displayed in public areas of various US cities. Her preferred medium is acrylic, although she also works in watercolor. Mary Ellen's art includes wall murals inspired by nature, and her designs have been used on puzzles, plates, cross-stitch patterns, and cards. She currently creates art and teaches in Texas. Visit her website at http://www.maryellenwehrli.com.

Photographers

ELISHA BUNTING is an employee of Best Friends Animal Society and works at the Bunny House.

BEVERLY ENDSLEY, a professional artist, volunteers with the Colorado House Rabbit Society.

VALERIE J. FOX adopted Baron from Brambley Hedge Rabbit Rescue.

CAROLINE GILBERT is the founder and manager of The Fund for Animals Rabbit Sanctuary.

STEPHEN GUIDA is a volunteer with Brambley Hedge Rabbit Rescue.

COURTNEY MCCARTY JOHNSON was a volunteer with the House Rabbit Society.

O. EARL MCCULLOUGH regularly photographs rabbits for the Colorado House Rabbit Society.

JOHN M. MEAD is involved in animal rescue. (A big "thank you" also to his special young helpers: Olivia, McKenna, and Milan Nelson and Elora Palmer.)

CLAY MYERS is senior photographer at Best Friends Animal Society and does freelance photography of nature and companion animals (cdune.1@email.com).

VELLY OLIVER is a freelance photographer who regularly photographs rabbits for Brambley Hedge Rabbit Rescue.

BILL REED, of Bill Reed Photography, specializes in portraits and lives in the Phoenix metro area.

RAY SILJA has adopted rabbits from Brambley Hedge Rabbit Rescue.

MICHAEL STEIN has adopted rabbits from the Colorado House Rabbit Society.

DEBBY WIDOLF is manager of the Bunny House at Best Friends Animal Society.

Organizations

Representatives of the following organizations answered my query for stories.

BEST FRIENDS ANIMAL SOCIETY: Special thanks to Elisha Bunting, Chandra Forsythe, Faith Maloney, Lena Sullivan, and Debby Widolf.

Best Friends Animal Society is a 501(c)(3) non-profit organization whose mission is driven by the simple philosophy that kindness to animals helps build a better world for all of us. The organization's sanctuary is located in southern Utah and is home to approximately 1,500 dogs, cats, horses, rabbits, birds, and other animals. In addition, Best Friends:

- promotes humane education in schools and with the public
- manages a model No More Homeless Pets program with shelters and humane groups in Utah to ensure that every healthy dog and cat is guaranteed a loving home
- assists with rescue efforts through the Best Friends Network and works with humane groups across the country to bring about a time when there are no more homeless pets
- reaches across the nation, helping individuals, humane groups, and entire communities set up spay/neuter, shelter, foster, and adoption programs
- publishes *Best Friends Magazine.*

Contact information: 5001 Angel Canyon Road, Kanab, UT 84741; 435-644-2001. Website: http://www.best-friends.org. E-mail: rabbits@bestfriends.org and bfnetwork@bestfriends.org.

BRAMBLEY HEDGE RABBIT RESCUE: Special thanks to Terry I. Bankert, Brock K. Dezelon, Kimberly K. Dezelon, Valerie J. Fox, Stephen Guida, Erika Smith Royal, Stacey Shirer, and Ray Silja.

Brambley Hedge Rabbit Rescue is a 501(c)(3) non-profit organization that has cared for abused, abandoned, and unwanted domestic rabbits since 1986. It is an all-volunteer, climate-controlled indoor shelter with supervised open-air play space. It houses approximately 75 rabbits at any time.

Over its first 20 years, the organization has placed more than 2,000 rabbits with caring adoptive parents. Brambley Hedge assists rabbits in various ways:

- arranging for volunteers to work with county agencies to check on abuse situations
- providing humane traps to the general public for capturing stray rabbits
- offering rabbit-care classes at the Arizona Humane Society
- participating in many Phoenix-area adoptathons to promote humane education and proper rabbit care
- disseminating additional information through their quarterly newsletter, "The Carrot Connection."

Contact information: P.O. Box 54506, Phoenix, AZ 85078-4506. Hopline (480) 443-3990. Website: http://www.bhrabbitrescue.org. E-mail: brambley2@bhrabbitrescue.org.

HOUSE RABBIT SOCIETY: Special thanks to Karalee Curry, Beverly W. Endsley, Kay G. Fritzsche, Courtney McCarty Johnson, Dr. Jerry LaBonde, Bea LeNoir, and Michael J. Stein.

The House Rabbit Society (HRS) is an international, volunteer-based, 501(c)(3) nonprofit organization. Their mission is twofold:

1. through their fostering program, volunteers rescue abandoned rabbits and find permanent adoptive homes for them
2. through education, they seek to reduce the number of unwanted rabbits—and to improve bunnies' lives—by helping people better appreciate these often misunderstood companion animals.

Since it was founded in 1988, HRS foster parents across the U.S. have rescued more than 15,000 rabbits. HRS neuters/spays all incoming rabbits, obtains necessary veterinary care for the bunnies, and attends to their social needs.

Having learned a tremendous amount about rabbits' social, behavioral, and medical requirements (compiled from existing data and necropsy reports), HRS helps veterinarians, humane societies, and individuals living with rabbits solve behavior and health problems, primarily through their website and membership publication, the *House Rabbit Journal*.

HRS chapters, educators, and foster families are found across the U.S. and, as of this printing, in Canada, Australia, Italy, Hong Kong, and Singapore.

Contact information for the national headquarters: 148 Broadway, Richmond, CA 94804; 510-970-7575. Website: http://www.rabbit.org. E-mail addresses: X@rabbit.org where "X" is any of the following: care, health, socialization, litter-training, chewing, digging, behavior, wildrehab, membership, or volunteer. Please click on FAQS and check the information on the website before e-mailing a question. In addition to the national website, chapter websites provide information on a variety of subjects.

THE FUND FOR ANIMALS RABBIT SANCTUARY: Special thanks to Caroline Gilbert and Patrice Pruitte.

The Fund for Animals Rabbit Sanctuary was established in 1978 by Caroline Gilbert, who worked with animal activist Cleveland Amory to establish a sanctuary specifically for domestic rabbits, providing a natural environment safe from predators. She devotes her 30-acre farm in Simpsonville, South Carolina, to the work of The Fund for Animals, a 501(c)(3) nonprofit organization. The sanctuary:

- has a unique "Home for Life" policy that ensures a permanent residence for approximately 50 rabbits, all fugitives from local shelters, commercial breeders, laboratories, and unfit homes
- provides advice on living with rabbits as companion animals
- publishes the "Rabbit Sanctuary Newsletter," which contains information about the resident rabbits and events at the sanctuary as well as health-related articles
- offers participants in the Adopt-a-Rabbit Sponsorship Program (virtual adoption) a certificate of adoption (good for one year), a color photograph and brief history of the sponsored rabbit, periodic newsletters, and an invitation to attend the sanctuary's annual "Picnic with the Rabbits."

Contact information: P.O. Box 80036, Simpsonville, SC 29680. Website: http://www.adopt-a-rabbit.org. E-mail: adoptarabbit@hotmail.com.

RESOURCES

Please note that web and e-mail addresses may change,
requiring an Internet search for current information.

RABBIT RESCUE ORGANIZATIONS

There are too many organizations to list here, and any list will periodically change. The House Rabbit Society maintains one of the most complete listings of national and international rabbit rescue groups, and other organizations have links to good resources too. If you don't have access to the web, perhaps the reference librarian at your local library will provide assistance.

Here are some organizations to get you started.

Best Friends Animal Society, 5001 Angel Canyon Road, Kanab, UT 84741
http://www.bestfriends.org

Brambley Hedge Rabbit Rescue, P.O. Box 54506, Phoenix, AZ 85078-4506
http://www.bhrabbitrescue.org

Cats & Rabbits & More, P.O. Box 212736, Chula Vista, CA 91921
http://www.catsandrabbitsandmore.com

Evergreen Rabbit Rescue, P.O. Box 2043, Woodinville, WA 98072-2043
http://www.evergreenrabbit.org

House Rabbit Resource Network, P.O. Box 152432, Austin, TX 78715
http://www.rabbitresource.org

House Rabbit Society (national headquarters), 148 Broadway, Richmond, CA 94804
http://www.rabbit.org

Rabbits' Rest Sanctuary (domestic rabbits), part of WildRescue, Inc. (wild rabbit rehabilitation), 4422 Cordova Ln., McKinney, TX 75070
http://www.rescuedrabbits.org

The Fund for Animals Rabbit Sanctuary, P.O. Box 80036, Simpsonville, SC 29680
http://www.adopt-a-rabbit.org

ADDITIONAL RESOURCES

There is not enough space here to list all the resources available for learning about rabbits. Access reputable websites, resource sections of other books, and representatives of your local rabbit rescue organization for additional references and recent publications.

BOOKS

House Rabbit Handbook: How to Live with an Urban Rabbit (4th Edition), Marinell Harriman. Drollery Press, 2005.

A House Rabbit Primer: Understanding and caring for your companion rabbit, Lucile C. Moore. Santa Monica Press, 2005.

Rabbit Health in the 21st Century: A Guide for Bunny Parents (Second Edition), Kathryn R. Smith. iUniverse, 2003.

Rabbit Secrets: A Comprehensive Owner's Guide, Maitland Sinclair. E-book available through PsyTech, Inc. (http://www.psytechpublishing.com).

Rabbits for Dummies, Audrey Pavia. Wiley Publishing Inc., 2003.

The Relaxed Rabbit: Massage for Your Pet Bunny, Chandra Moira Beal. iUniverse, Inc., 2004.

Stories Rabbits Tell: A Natural and Cultural History of a Misunderstood Creature, Susan E. Davis and Margo DeMello. Lantern Books, 2003.

What Your Rabbit Needs, Betsy Sikora Siino. A Dorling Kindersley Book, 2000.

Why Does My Rabbit…? Anne McBride. Souvenir Press, Ltd., 1998.

MEDICAL TEXTS AND HEALTH-RELATED WEBSITES

BSAVA Manual of Rabbit Medicine and Surgery, Paul Flecknell (ed.). British Small Animal Veterinary Association, 2000.

Biology of Rabbits and Rodents, The (Fourth Edition), John E. Harkness and Joseph E. Wagner. Lea & Febiger, 1995.

Ferrets, Rabbits, and Rodents: Clinical Medicine and Surgery (Second Edition), Katherine E. Quesenberry and James W. Carpenter (eds.). Saunders, 2004.

Notes on Rabbit Internal Medicine, Ron Rees Davies and Richard Saunders, Jr. Blackwell Publishing, Inc., 2005.

Rabbit and Rodent Dentistry Handbook, Vittorio Capello, DVM, with Margherita Gracis, DVM. Zoological Education Network, 2005.

Textbook of Rabbit Medicine, Frances Harcourt-Brown. Butterworth-Heinemann, 2002.

INTERNET RESOURCES
- House Rabbit Society: http://www.rabbit.org (especially the links to Care, Behavior, Health, FAQS, and Chapters)
- MediRabbit: http://www.medirabbit.com
- Morfz: http://www.morfz.com or http://home-page.mac.com/mattocks/morfz (click on Rabbit References and Rabbit Veterinarians)
- Rabbit Adoption and Information Network: http://www.lagomorphs.com (click on Rabbit Adoption and Information Network)
- Veterinary Partner: http://www.veterinarypartner.com

OTHER READINGS
HUMAN-ANIMAL RELATIONSHIPS
Many wonderful books have been written about relationships between humans and other species. The following list, although not comprehensive, suggests some excellent authors on this topic: Allen and Linda Anderson; Marc Beckoff; Jack Canfield and Mark Victor Hansen (*Chicken Soup* anthologies); Michael W. Fox; Jane Goodall; Amelia Kinkade; Gary Kowalski; Joanne Lauck; Jeffrey Masson; Susan Chernak McElroy; Mary Lou Randour; Tom Regan; Allen Schoen; Kenneth Shapiro; Penelope Smith; Kim Stallwood; and Michael Tobias.

DEATH, DYING, AND GRIEF
Blessing the Bridge: What Animals Teach Us about Death, Dying, and Beyond, Rita Reynolds. NewSage Press, 2001.

Goodbye, Friend: Healing Wisdom for Anyone Who Has Ever Lost a Pet, Gary Kowalski. Stillpoint Publishing, 1997.

Pet Loss: A Spiritual Guide, Julia Harris. Lantern Books, 2002.

Rainbows & Bridges: An Animal Companion Memorial Kit, Allen and Linda Anderson. New World Library, 2005.

When Only the Love Remains: The Pain of Pet Loss, Emily Margaret Stuparyk. Hushion House Publishing, Ltd., 2000.

MAGAZINES AND OTHER PUBLICATIONS
Best Friends Animal Society, Brambley Hedge Rabbit Rescue, the House Rabbit Society, and The Fund for Animals Rabbit Rescue (see information on previous pages) each produce a publication.

Critters U.S.A. and *Rabbits U.S.A.* (annual magazines), BowTie, Inc., P.O. Box 57900, Los Angeles, CA 90057 http://www.animalnetwork.com (select "Small Animals")

Fur & Feather (monthly magazine), Printing for Pleasure Ltd., Elder House, Chattisham, Ipswich, Suffolk IP8 3QE, UK
http://www.furandfeather.co.uk

laJoie: The Journal That Honors All Beings (quarterly publication). LaJoie and Company, P.O. Box 145, Batesville, VA 22924
lajoieco1@aol.com

Luv Notes (newsletter), BunnyLuv Rabbit Resource Center, 16742 Stagg Street, #104, Van Nuys, CA 91406
http://www.bunnyluv.org

Rabbit Tracks (newsletter), P.O. Box 2602, Woburn, MA 01888-1102 http://www.rabbitnetwork.org

WEB DISCUSSION LISTS

Disabled rabbits' health and care:
http://groups.yahoo.com/group/disabledrabbits

EtherBun: A moderated list regarding health, behavior, and care of companion rabbits.
http://www.bio.miami.edu/hare

Rabbit Welfare Association: Improving the quality of life for companion rabbits in the United Kingdom. RWF, P.O. Box 603, Horsham, West Sussex, RH13 5WL, United Kingdom. National helpline: 0870-046-5249.
http://www.rabbitwelfare.co.uk

There are additional web lists that may be of interest. For example, the House Rabbit Society provides links for people who want to chat, who live in other countries, etc. There are some comprehensive indexes listed, too. Go to http://www.rabbit.org and access Links.

PRODUCTS AND SUPPLIES

American Pet Diner: The Healthy Hay Products Company, HC 62, Box 62505, Eureka, NV 89316. 775-237-5570, 800-656-2691
http://www.americanpetdiner.com

Bunny Bytes: P.O. Box 1581, Kent, WA 98035. 888-563-9300 (A fax phone; it will beep before the voice mail message.)
http://www.bunnybytes.com

Bunny Heaven: PMB 262, 16 Mt. Bethel Rd., Warren, NJ 07059-5604. 732-563-1904
http://www.bunnyheaven.com

BunnyLuv Essentials: 16742 Stagg Street, #104, Van Nuys, CA 91406. 818-988-4488
http://www.bunnyluv.com

The Busy Bunny: P.O. Box 1023, San Bruno, CA 94066-7023. 877-992-8669, 650-872-2920
http://www.busybunny.com

House Rabbit Resource Network: P.O. Box 152432, Austin, TX 78715. 512-444-3277
http://www.rabbitresource.org

House Rabbit Society (many chapters sell items): http://www.rabbit.org ("Chapters")

Leith Petwerks, Inc.: P.O. Box 453, Gosport, IN 47433. 800-956-3576
http://www.leithpetwerks.com

Oxbow Enterprises: 29012 Mill Road, Murdock, NE 68407. 800-249-0366
http://www.oxbowhay.com

Rabbit Adoption and Information Network (maintains a list of suppliers):
http://lagomorphs.com

SERVICES
Guardian Campaign: In Defense of Animals, 3010 Kerner Blvd., San Rafael, CA 94901. 415-388-9641
http://www.idausa.org

Professional Pet Transports, Inc.: 59154 Trafton Lane, John Day, OR 97845. 866-273-7387
http://www.pro-pet-transports.com

CRUELTY-FREE PRODUCTS AND DISSECTION ALTERNATIVE PROGRAM
Several organizations offer informative shopping guides to help consumers choose cruelty-free products that have not been tested on animals. In addition, many of the groups provide an alternative to the science class requirement of killing and/or performing dissections on animals, such as workbooks, software, and models to promote effective learning about animal biology and anatomy.

Some organizations to contact are:

American Anti-Vivisection Society (AAVS): 801 Old York Rd., Suite 204, Jenkintown, PA 19046. 215-887-0816
http://www.aavs.org

National Anti-Vivisection Society (NAVS): 53 W. Jackson Blvd., Suite 1552, Chicago, IL 60604. 800-888-NAVS (6287)
http://www.navs.org

New England Anti-Vivisection Society (NEAVS): 333 Washington St., Suite 850, Boston, MA 02108. 617-523-6020
http://www.neavs.org
(Contact the Ethical Science and Education Coalition at that same address and telephone number for free science education tools.)

People for the Ethical Treatment of Animals (PETA): 501 Front St., Norfolk, VA 23510. 757-622-7382
http//www.peta.org

Index

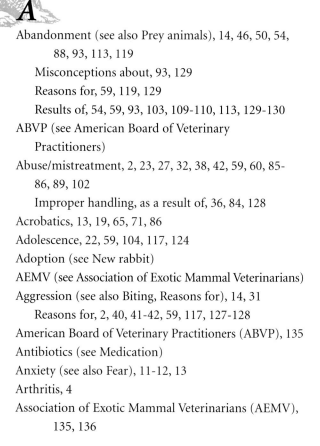

G

Gastrointestinal stasis, 2, 7
Grieving (see Companionship, Loss/death)
Grooming (see Cleaning a rabbit; Fur)
Guardian (as preferred term for "owner"), xviii, 124

H

Handling, 2, 33, 34, 36, 73, 76, 84, 125, 128
Hay, alfalfa (see Feeding)
Hay, grass (see Feeding)
Head tilt (due to neurological damage), 32, 34
Holiday concerns, 82
House Rabbit Society, 10, 38, 59, 63, 107, 140
Housing (see also Cages; Hutches; Litter box), 3, 18-19,
    125, 127-128
    Wire flooring, 2-3
Hutches (see also Arthritis; Cages; Housing), 23, 27

I

Illness (see Medical care)
Injury (see Medical care)

J

Jumping (see Acrobatics)

L

LaRoche, Nancy, 37, 118
Lennox, Dr. Angela M., 134, 136
Litter box (see also Housing; Spay/neuter), 17, 125
    Litter/cedar shavings, 2, 125
Litter training (see also Spay/neuter), 17, 112, 117

M

Make Mine Chocolate!™ campaign, 59
McElroy, Susan Chernak, xxiv, 18, 136-137
Medical care (see also Medication; Teeth;
    Veterinarians), 38, 61, 68-69, 131, 134-135
    Anesthesia, 117
    Companionship, importance of, 71
    Emergency care, 61, 86, 89, 93, 101, 110, 121,
        124, 131
    Mites, ear, 60
    Mites, fur, 60, 85
    Parasites, 50
    Surgery, fasting before, 132
    Symptoms of illness/injury, 1-2, 21, 47, 95, 101, 102,
        109, 115, 128
Medication
    Antibiotics, 21, 132
    Bicillin injections, 61, 62, 64
    Pain relief, 132
Moore, Lucile C., 131, 137

N

Neglect (see Abuse/mistreatment)
Neuter (see Reproduction; Spay/neuter)
New rabbit, 104, 123

O

Overpopulation (see Reproduction)

P

Pain, 2, 4, 5, 131, 132, 134

Pairing rabbits (see also Social Nature), 10-11, 14, 29-31, 103

Personality/true nature (see also Companionship; Prey animals; Social nature), xx, 7, 9, 27, 40, 86, 87, 110, 115, 129

    Exhibitions of, 13, 26, 35, 39, 51, 53, 56, 58, 67, 69-70, 85, 102-103, 104, 111, 119-120

    Innate qualities, xxiii, 56, 117, 127

    True nature, uncaged rabbits, 14-17, 28, 44, 58-59, 78-82, 83-84

Petting zoos (see County fairs)

Physiology, 36

    Physical impairment, 2, 4, 27, 32, 33, 84

Play (see also Companionship; Social nature), 124, 125

Predators, 14, 19, 27, 46, 54, 55, 71, 93, 102, 113, 126

    Protecting babies from, 97, 117

Prey animals (see also Abandonment), 13, 91, 92, 93, 113, 126, 127

    Illness/injury, signs of, 128

    Psychology of, 13, 40, 123, 126

Purchasing (see New rabbit; Self-education)

Purring, tooth, 33, 39, 51, 74

R

Reproduction (see also Adolescence; Spay/neuter), 50, 53, 100, 115, 117, 119

    Nest building, 115

    Overpopulation, rapidity of, 94, 99, 100

Rescue, 14, 46-47, 54-55, 88-92, 94-99, 100, 110, 113-115, 118, 130

S

Safety (see also Bunny-proofing), 127

School/classroom, rabbit in, xxiii, xxiv, 1, 2, 41, 42, 85-86, 87, 126-130

Self-education (about rabbit care), 104, 133

Sexual maturity (see Adolescence; Reproduction; Spay/neuter)

Siegel, Dr. Bernie, xxiv, 54, 137

Sight (see Vision)

Social nature (see also Companionship; Personality/true nature), xx, 11, 22, 29, 31, 40, 48, 71, 124, 129

Spay/neuter (see also Reproduction), 53, 100, 112, 117, 124, 132

    Benefits of, 17, 117, 124

Splay leg, 6

Stress (see also Fear; School/classroom, rabbit in), 12, 13, 27, 73, 77, 82, 91, 96, 108, 128

T

Teeth (see also Chewing; Medical care; Purring, Tooth), 127, 134

    Abscess, 60, 61, 62, 68, 69, 134

    Malocclusion, 134, 135

    Problems, treatment of, 93, 134-135

Testing, product, rabbits as victims of, xx

Thumping (hind feet), 7, 11-12, 16, 20

U

Urine burn, 4, 6, 32, 60

V

Veterinarians (see also Medical care), 53, 117, 124, 128,
        131-133, 134-135
    Rabbits as exotics, 128, 131, 135
Vision, 7, 11, 49
    Biting, as related to, 49
    Scanning, 23, 49

Nova Maris Press

Nova Maris Press is dedicated to contributing positively to the planet and its citizens. We value our readers and encourage your feedback, suggestions, and ideas. To request a copy of this book or to be added to our mailing list, please contact us at:

Nova Maris Press
977 Seminole Trail, #356
Charlottesville, VA 22901-2824
www.novamarispress.com